Avoided No More

AVOIDED NO MORE

On Writing Through Struggle, Shame, and Self-Doubt

An Open Book Company Anthology

Edited By Kim Marsh

Plymouth James Press

Plymouth James Press
An imprint of The Open Book Company

First Edition

Library of Congress Cataloguing-in-Publication Data Available Upon Request

Paperback ISBN: 978-1-970635-00-3
e-Book ISBN: 978-1-970635-01-0

Edited by Kim Marsh
Cover Design and Book Icon by Deja Brown
Text Design by Nicki Pappas

To all the "I'm working on a novel"-ists, sometimes-journalers, starry-eyed storytellers, notebook scrawlers, and nighttime poets.

Contents

Since when did telling our own stories and deriving their insights become so reviled?

— Melissa Febos, *Body Work*

Introduction

THE STORIES CONTAINED WITHIN THIS ANTHOLOGY WERE AL-most never written. Some of them were ideas scrawled on scraps of paper, lines collecting dust, half-completed thoughts in emails and notebooks; some on post-its left crumpled at the bottom of tote bags.

Some of these stories were ghosts of long-lost memories, haunting the authors daily, while others were mere fleeting thoughts. Some settled right beneath the surface, others buried deep, deep within; it took a lot of work to excavate each sentence from the rubble.

For some of our contributing authors, the spotlight now shines in triumph. For others, discomfort. A handful of them have been previously published; for some, it's their first time in print. Some may refer to themselves as "aspiring writers" and others as "experienced authors." None of these self-ascribed labels are particularly relevant in this context. To me, and to these previously blank pages, they are all brave storytellers.

The idea for this anthology came to me two years ago, like a bolt out of the blue. I was cozy in bed with a book, a beautiful personal essay collection featuring a variety of authors. I wondered what the authors thought (and felt) about publishing such vulnerable stories in print. (Often, we assume "published writers" are "real writers" and "real writers" must be confident as hell, right?) Another thought quickly entered my mind: "I bet the writers in my writing community could do something like this…"

The idea for curating and editing my own collection of essays began to flicker in my mind. But what would be the unifying topic?

Lightbulb on.

The next morning, I emailed the writers in my virtual writing community to invite them to participate in this fledgling project. And I did something a little mean. Cruel almost. You see, I asked a bunch of writers to write about something they'd been *avoiding writing about*. That's right. The unifying topic of my essay collection would be the stories these writers had put off telling. Swore they'd never touch. Avoided like the plague. What were they scared of facing on the page? I wanted to know. Oh, and I also wanted them to write *about* the writing (my favorite prompt as a writing coach). Not only did I ask them to dig deep and pull out whatever they could find; I also wanted them to tell me how awful it was in the process.

"Go to a place of discomfort, but not pain," I advised. "It's a bit like working out…find that edge." Right on cue, the struggle, shame, self-doubt, fear and inner critic came roaring back in response. (By the way, I was not exempt. My own essay is included in these pages, too!) Almost immediately, like clockwork, the mental "What if?" gymnastics from all of us began. *What if I'm not good enough? What if my writing isn't good enough? What if my story isn't interesting enough? What if no one cares about what I have to say? What if my mom really cares about what I have to say? What if this is just too exposing or too honest? What if no one reads it? What if everyone reads it?*

These questions—and so many related others—are exactly why this book exists. So, we've included them! In this anthology, you will read 14 essays from 14 writers. At the end of each essay, you'll find a special Behind-the-Scenes companion piece; it's there to provide a peek into each author's thoughts, feelings and reflections about writing and publishing the piece you've just read.

Now, most introductions to books include some clues to let you know if you're in the right place. Either directly or indirectly, they tell you who the book you're reading is actually for. It's an opportunity for a moment of pause before you dive in. Are you sure you got on the right train? Do you know where this thing is headed?

As a result of its structure, this anthology runs the risk of having a bit of an identity crisis. There are a few potential journeys you can take with this book and, as such, it might be confusing to know if the ticket you purchased is leading you where you think it is. So, let's address who may be on board with you and all the routes we'll cover.

Maybe you're here because you find resonance, comfort or insight in hearing from others. It can be helpful to know we're not alone. The subjects within this collection vary widely. In one essay, we hear the story of someone grappling with her racial identity; in another, a firsthand view into the shattered hopes of a future in academia. Other essays cover topics like mental health, family dynamics, divorce, neurodivergence, sexuality, grief, religion and more. You may not find yourself aligned with every writer's point of view but may benefit from exploring what arises inside of you as you expose yourself to the lived experiences of others.

Maybe you're here because you recognize that struggle, shame and self-doubt are universal. Writing is not the only way we tell our stories and lay ourselves bare. There are loads of avenues for vulnerability and honesty in this life. The inner critic spares few, and we believe there's some universality to the fear writers face when unmasking themselves to the world.

Or, possibly you're here because you love a good, juicy tell-all. You are absolutely welcome here. There is no sugar-coating within these pages. If you want the raw truth, you'll get it!

And, finally, perhaps you're here because you consider yourself a writer. An aspiring writer. A wannabe writer. A published (or unpublished) author. A "I used to love writing as a kid" person. An avid reader who thinks, "maybe someday I would..." The family storyteller. A blogger. Someone who journals but doesn't know "if I could ever share my writing with anyone." A writer. Just a writer.

Here, we believe you'll find a feeling of camaraderie with these essayists. In some ways, every Behind-the-Scenes reflection is a love letter to another writer. Because I wanted to remind all of us—

The contributing authors,

You, dear reader,

And myself—

That we can struggle, feel shame, encounter self-doubt and still do the thing anyway.

Still post. Still pitch. Still show up. Still read aloud. Still share. Still publish. Still grab the mic. Still tell our stories. Still tell the truth. Still tell our truth.

Still write.

Still write.

Still write.

Please, for the love of everything, still write. Keep writing. Write *through* it all, *because* of it all, *with* it all, and *about* it all.

So, whether you're grabbing the popcorn and a tissue box or your pen and favorite notebook, this book is for you. After all, we bookend our collection with two stories that speak to the power of being seen.

Ultimately, all of these essays (and their behind-the-scenes companions) are here to remind us that none of us are alone on this journey—as writers, as truthtellers, or as humans. There's a vulnerability to being seen, and being seen on the page—no takebacks—can leave one feeling particularly tender. On behalf of all of the contributing authors, I'd like to thank you for being here. Thank you for bearing witness. Thank you for seeing us.

The stories you're about to read have long been avoided. But they are now ready to see the light. Whether you consider yourself a writer or not, our hope is that perhaps through the reading of *our* truths, you may find you are ready to flip the switch on some of your own.

—Kim Marsh
November 2025

A Note:
The stories contained within this book cover a range of topics including grief and loss, abuse, childhood and religious trauma, and more. Please proceed with care.

You're Blushing!

By Federica Bruniera

GUSTS OF WIND MAKE THE SAND TWIRL AND DANCE IN THE campground as the sun progressively disappears behind the hills. It's not even 6 p.m., but I'm already inside my car—which doubles as my house—trying to get some work done, while the Patagonian weather goes all in, shaking the world around like a snow globe. A knock on the window. I flinch. The nice lady from the campervan two trees away invites me to the workshop she and her family are about to host at the local cultural center.

That would be so cool, I think. *A glimpse into the local culture while making travel friends. It would be fun, a little adventure after a few days of driving long hours talking only to myself. But wait… What kind of workshop is it? What if I have to be in front of strangers doing things or talking? I'll have to introduce myself all over again. I'm tired, I can't control when I'll be back, and it will probably get overwhelming…*

With a gentle smile, I say I have other plans (a bold-faced lie) and turn down the kind offer.

The next morning I'm leaving. I can't bring myself to go knock on the door and do the right thing. I consider waiting around for a little while, hoping for someone to get out of the van so I'm able to say my goodbyes. I tiptoe out of the campground instead, as much as the loud engine of my car allows me to, and I'm on my way. I'll probably never see them again.

Really, Federica, how hard can knocking on a damn door be? What's the worst thing that could have happened there? They were such a nice family. Congratulations. Now you can add them to the ever-growing list of people who probably think you're rude, cold, and heartless.

———

The green door of the little family restaurant is open. Without slowing down, as if that was not my intended destination, I take a peek inside as I pass. It's full and brimming with conversation as usual. I stop on the sidewalk, fidgeting, pretending to fix my hair, checking my phone. Anything to delay the dreaded moment in which I'll open the door and all eyes will be on me for a split second. I'll have to greet the room and desperately look for a spot at one of the four tables. I breathe and step in, mumbling a "Buenas tardes," and proceed to squeeze my body against the wall. I remain there until my partner arrives and I can be a shadow again.

I hate entering places first. Sometimes I linger outside shops that catch my attention until someone else goes inside, and I can trail behind like a little dog.

If you think anyone bothers actually looking at you, you're flattering yourself. Nobody cares, so don't be a crybaby and just enter the damn restaurant! Where's the strong, independent woman you always claim to be?

———

I don't go out alone too much in the village. In the cobbled streets, there's nowhere to hide. People gather on wooden benches on the sidewalk, sit on colorful rocking chairs in front of their constantly opened front doors, stop for a chat at every corner, while kids ride their bicycles or run around in shouting little gangs. Village-crowded is the kind of crowded that doesn't make you invisible enough and doesn't excuse you from greeting people, even if they're just faces without a name. So when I do have to go out, I walk around, gaze firmly on the ground, carefully choosing the emptier streets, looking around every now and then hoping for my smile to be warm enough to hide the discomfort of feeling like an eternal outsider. I know there's no neon sign above my head, and I know I'm not that different from anybody around here despite being the only foreigner. Yet I can't help but feel like a bent screw sticking out of a wooden board.

You never lift your gaze from the ground. After all these years, you still can't recognize your neighbors. You barely leave the house. It's no wonder you can't integrate in the community.

———

I'm in my room, ear against the door, trying to pick up any sound coming from down the hall. Silence. I carefully turn the knob, tiptoe down the stairs barefoot, check left and right. The way to the fridge is clear. I sprint towards it, grab a peach yoghurt with one hand and a spoon with the other. I backtrack like a thief to my room, to safety. A sigh of relief. Another day, another breakfast earned without having to greet another "hostile" soul good morning. The "Skillful Ninja Run to the Kitchen," heart pounding in my chest, is one of the techniques that serve me better. I've perfected it over the years, from university dorms to flats with roommates to renting a room in a stranger's house.

No free access to the fridge? Sounds like a great weight loss method. You should trademark it. Or maybe you should trademark your stupidity; is a minute of chitchat really that hard?

———

I've just moved across the ocean, and I know nobody in town but him. He's why I moved in the first place. He brings me to parties with his friends and then leaves me in the middle of a stranger's living room for minutes on end while he goes for a smoke, or to the bathroom, or to get whatever from the kitchen. Therefore, I proceed to find myself a corner and stay there, casually sipping my drink, with an awkward smile on my face and tears in the corners of my eyes. Some people come to have a chat for a couple of minutes and ask generic, harmless questions and then move on. At some parties, games are involved: I especially hate the ones that single you out and put you on the spot, anything from miming things to drawing stuff, to coming up quickly with a story, a word, a compliment, a question. No matter how easy the task, I simply can't stand the pressure and the perceived judgment of a room full of strangers.

If TikTok had existed back then, you could have launched the trend of "panic attacks in strangers' bathrooms before putting on your most composed face again and pretending nothing had happened." Good thing you never wear make-up. It would never last.

———

In school, I was the smart kid. I never feared the infamous parent-teacher meetings because I had good grades and a non-disruptive personality. One thing my teachers never failed to point out, however, was how I should speak up more in class and "show my talents," as they could benefit and be an inspiration to others. *Yeah, right. As if inspiring one another was a thing teenagers were concerned about.* I wonder if those teachers ever felt their heart jumping out of their chest, their whole body sweating, their voice trembling, and their face on fire every time they raised their hand or were forced to speak in class. I know they meant well and wanted to see me shine and unleash my full potential; however, they were not the ones embarrassed and soul-crushed on a daily basis. Plus, they didn't seem to even take notice whenever my cheeks started burning and the genius class-mate of the day shouted: "Uuh, you're blushing!" Wow, smartass, I hadn't realized! Thanks to this life-saving re-mark, I will now switch off my balloon-looking red face—something that's totally within my control—and proceed to dig my own grave in this very classroom floor.

In middle school, my male classmates were pretty cruel and ruthless, but I was never bullied. Teachers used to say that, despite my being quiet and shy, I managed somehow to make them respect me. Sure, if the definition of respect is "a well-crafted talent at making myself invisible," then I guess you could call it that. It's funny how adults some-times really don't have a clue. Invisibility can happen in plain sight; you just have to make yourself small and unin-teresting enough so that people will ignore you or forget about you even when you are right there in the room. I wasn't bullied simply because the bullies in my class only remembered me when they needed to copy their home-work.

Uninteresting is okay. A girl's got to do what a girl's got to do to survive.

———

The way my mum used to reinforce my quiet "thank-yous" whenever I received gifts was not lost on me. Her most re-iterated comments to me were probably "go say hi," "say goodbye properly," and "say thanks like you mean it." But when I say things, I *do* mean them. In my constant struggle to find the right words, saying something—anything—out loud is already a big deal. It's just surprisingly difficult to show flashy emotions, big enthusiasm or affection. "People can't read your mind, you need to say what you think," she would remind me. But what if I don't have the words? What if, when put on the spot, my mind freezes and goes blank, like a puppet whose strings have just been cut? Why couldn't anyone ever consider the struggle for a second?

You're on your own, kid.

———

I didn't have a name for it until I was 30. I figured that gluing my ear to my dorm room waiting for the hall to clear in order to avoid social interaction was not exactly what most people would define as "normal," but, well…it was just a thing I did. Plus, I never really bought into the normal vs. abnormal dichotomy anyway.

There is a tendency to think about social anxiety as panic attacks in social situations, but the truth is that it comes in many shapes and forms. I know labels are only helpful to organize and categorize the reality we live in and do not necessarily define or limit us as human beings, but when I got that label it felt like an elephant-sized rock was lifted from my chest. Because it meant that there was someone else out there who could relate to what I had been feeling all my life.

The "social anxiety" label doesn't make it any easier to navigate a reality made for extroverts, but now I can accept it and, for the most part, embrace it as a part of me. Now I can show up to in-person or virtual events with my anti-stress pillowcase without shame, I can readily respond if someone points out that I'm blushing, and I can say "no" to situations that may be particularly anxiety-inducing.

Social anxiety is like playing a board game in which you know the gameplay really well, you highly fear the consequences, and the rules are constantly changing. I can be sociable one day and completely withdrawn the next. I know that sometimes I have to go out of my way and embrace the discomfort if the occasion is worth it. I know I can't expect people to understand, and that many are judgmental of some behaviors—not out of sheer meanness, but because they just can't relate to social anxiety in any way.

I'm often asked why I travel so much, why I can't stay in a place for too long. I've always thought it was simple wanderlust and a thirst for the beautifully unknown, but maybe it's that perfect balance between the almost constant need for novelty and the possibility of satisfying this need in a space where there are no strings attached. I'd rather be the spider, weaving my own strings from a safe space, than the prey, risking finding myself trapped in a web where I'm expected to be and behave in a certain way.

Putting myself in new situations, despite the inherent stress that comes with it, gives me the control I need over the kind of social interactions I want. A life on the road means that—aside from maybe the cashier at the grocery store or the campground owner—I can go without talking to people for days. This can be very isolating, but at the same time eliminates a layer of uncertainty and awkwardness that I am rarely ready to face. I think it is also a—maybe rather eccentric—way of having endless shots at trying to be someone else, someone who is sociable and confident, like a videogame with endless lives. It is a personal and resilient strategy for getting closer to a 2.0 version of myself.

So far I have failed, but the world is big, and I am not settling down any time soon.

Behind-the-Scenes

I've been staring at this empty document for an unreasonable amount of time. This Behind-the-Scenes is proving harder to write than the actual essay. And not because I am a particularly inspired or talented writer—even just defining myself as a "writer" still makes my inner critic roar with laughter—but rather because my essay wasn't supposed to be one in the first place. The piece came out of me in bits and pieces as a way to process my reality in retrospect after my diagnosis. As a person with social anxiety,

I have never been quite the talker (shockingly enough), and writing has always been my refuge and my way of expressing, even to myself, what I was feeling. This essay tried to get out of my being for a very long time. I could feel the words leaking out of my brain in disconnected sentences at random moments when I wasn't ready to give them space. When I finally opened the faucet and allowed the words to flow, they were full of sadness, frustration, and anger but also a source of great liberation. Written for my eyes only, the piece was devoid of any kind of pressure and felt like one of the best first drafts I had ever produced. I daresay I felt proud! For a blissful split second, I even thought that maybe I could use it as a manual of instructions to give to the people who don't get me, like a "fragile, handle with care" sticker on a cardboard box.

That feeling, however, did not last long; the minute I was given the opportunity to read my essay to someone else and possibly publish it, I decided it was crap. It was fragmented and confusing, the timeline was all over the place, and I sounded pathetic. At the same time, I wasn't nearly qualified enough to be writing about such a topic. Who did I think I was, lecturing people about what social anxiety is or is not? What an arrogant "writer" (cue scornful laughter) I was being.

Despite the positive feedback and encouragement from my writers' community, the editing process was a real struggle. I needed more examples to make my experience less of a farce and a clearer chronological order so that people wouldn't get lost. At each round of edits, I would come up with new issues that could expose the mediocrity of my writing and the irrelevance of my experience. At the same time, my fellow writers' essays—which I had not even read yet—sounded amazing, their topics so poignant, and their skill level light years away from mine. Sometimes I think that, hadn't the essay basically written itself, it would not exist today due to my resistance being so high.

I settled into quiet acceptance after letting it rest for a (long) while and coming to terms with my experience not having to be universal. The idea of showing a vulnerable part of myself and being judged by strangers and friends is still extremely uncomfortable and scary. I cannot help but wonder what my family will think: that I am an exaggerating attention-seeker, or that they could have done more, or perhaps that I should have learned to navigate life like a proper human being by now. However, when the overwhelm and the second-guessing get too intense, I try to ground myself by going back to my "why."

It may sound cheesy, but having a purpose puts everything into perspective. Why did I write this piece in the first place, before all the doubts and imposter syndrome? Because it was healing for the adult me, but also for the younger version of me who blushed in school and felt like dying every single time. Therefore, if just one person sees themselves in my words and doesn't feel as lonely in their experience, this essay deserves to be out in the world. Coming to peace with this doesn't make the experience of publishing it any easier, but sometimes the message is more important than the messenger's vanity, and fear of rejection needs to take the back seat for a possible greater good.

The final push that made me agree to this project was the realization that I trusted my editor and my co-writers deeply. Whenever I get compliments or positive feedback, my first thought is: "They're just being nice, they don't really mean it." If you trust your team, however, you start understanding that they want the best possible outcome for you, which translates into helping you create the best version of your work. I used to be very private with my writing, but now I share more; I ask for help a tiny bit more, and I trust their suggestions and opinions, praise included. If they believe in this essay, why shouldn't I?

So cheers to many more attempts and cheers to this first written "confession." It's for all the visible and invisible versions of myself and for all the other "mini-me-in-hiding" out there who haven't found their words yet.

It's Probably Nothing

By Laura Vegh

BREATHE, I THINK TO MYSELF.

You've got this. You've worked so much for this. Hours, days, weeks, months, years. All the effort you put in has gotten you here.

Breathe, I tell myself again. *You've got this. You can do this.*

I learned when I was very young that some people will be given everything on a silver platter. It doesn't matter how good or bad they are. They will get what they want with little to no effort because they are part of the right family, have enough money, or know the right people. But I also learned that you can make a path for yourself among these people. You may come from a less significant background or family or have less money. But if you find something you're good at and you work really hard, you can beat the odds.

Some say that's a naïve way of looking at life. Others think that it's incredibly optimistic. I was never an optimist. Though I can't say I wasn't naïve either. School was easy for me from an early age. While I was constantly reminded we're not all equal and privilege exists, I was also lucky enough that my hard work paid off. I was top of the class and excelled at everything I set my mind to.

University wasn't much different. It came with a fresh set of challenges, but I overcame every one of them. Learning was my passion, and I wanted to put it to good use. Upon graduation, I embarked on a journey that would change my life in more ways than I could've possibly imagined: I started a Ph.D. and got a job as a teaching assistant at the same university where I'd earned my bachelor's degree.

I often heard the life of young Ph.D. students was anything but easy. You had to work on your research, teach, help guide undergraduate students, write academic papers, and take care of the various admin tasks that are thrown your way. But I was passionate about it. I had chosen my research area—cybersecurity—carefully. I loved it and knew it was such an important topic; I believed my work could make a real impact. It was a bit of a unique path. In my department, nobody studied it, so I'd have to be alone in my research. That never scared me, though, so I started my work with a lot of hope and enthusiasm.

One September evening, just before the new academic year started, and with it my Ph.D. journey, I went out with a friend. Hearing about my new career path for the first time, she said, with an almost worried tone, "You know you won't be doing much research, right? You'll end up being your supervisor's secretary or worse…It's what all these guys want from Ph.D. students. Especially if you're a woman."

Nonsense, I thought to myself. Yes, I had heard these stories before. But I also knew that these types of incidents didn't happen all the time, and I was determined to focus on the bright side.

"I'm sure it won't be that bad," I replied after a few seconds of awkward silence. "I know people who've completed their Ph.D. in this department, and they never said anything like that. Maybe some supervisors are jerks, but mine's fine. Come on, you know him. He was your teacher too!"

She smiled, took a deep breath, then said, "All I'm saying is, be careful. Maybe keep an eye on other jobs too. It can't hurt."

I can't say for a fact what I felt at that moment, leaving that conversation. Annoyance at the unsolicited advice? Anger at all the preconceived ideas people have and at how they try to shove them down other people's throats? Whatever it was, I decided to give it no further thought. This was the right path for me. I could do it. I just knew it.

I've always had to fight hard to feel like I belong in a place, but the first year went surprisingly well. I advanced with my research far beyond my own expectations. I also started teaching and, despite the wild anxiety I felt, I got along with my students.

In hindsight, there were many red flags from the very beginning, but I was too focused on my work to notice. Since I was mostly working solo on my research, I had a schedule that didn't align quite well with the others. However, I was always sure to be there whenever there were team meetings and jumped to help when someone needed me. I'd have been more than happy to have others join me in my work, too. But that excitement was cut short pretty early on.

At one of my first official team meetings, as everyone was discussing their research and future projects, one of the members, the second in degree after the supervisor, looked at me and said, "What shall we do with you, Laura? There's not much use to your work for us."

Instead of helping me out, my supervisor laughed and said, "Yes, we'll have to work extra hard to integrate her."

Hearing a computer engineer claiming cybersecurity had no use was at least a bit weird. But I tried to consider it a joke and moved on. Despite that initial incident, in this environment overall, I felt like I was doing pretty well. So, one day, when my supervisor casually said to me, "You're not a team player, Laura. You don't really help me out around here. You need to help me out more often," I was shocked, especially since his feedback was coming right as I was supporting his team by doing something that had nothing to do with my research, or my job for that matter—arranging furniture in a hall before a conference.

Naively, I replied, "But...I'm here, I'm helping out. I've always been here when asked. If you ever want me to be more involved in other team activities, just let me know."

I don't remember his exact answer verbatim. But I do remember it sent chills down my spine. Every instinct in me was telling me something was off. And I should run as fast and as far as I could.

You're paranoid, Laura, I thought to myself. *He's a bit of a moron. He's also very tired and stressed. This conference is a nightmare to organize. It's probably nothing.*

It's probably nothing.

That thought…hopeful, innocent, naïve, and optimistic, followed me every day of my work there. But small red flags continued. A weird word here, an observation that was completely out of place there. Things taken out of context. *Probably nothing.*

Then one day, the funding for my work started disappearing. I was expected to continue to write papers and attend international conferences with costs that could easily reach $2,000 or more of my own money. All while representing the university and not my own interest. A paper of mine was approved soon after, but it would be up to me to figure out how to present it. "There simply aren't any more funds at the university. You don't have to publish now. You can postpone the research and finish a year later if you can't pay out of pocket," I was told.

A reasonable explanation, I thought, as I left my supervisor's office. His suggestion, however, was anything but reasonable. In Romania, where I was doing my Ph.D., extending the duration of your studies is not very well seen. Your Ph.D. is supposed to last three years. That's how long you can get funding. Anything over that will be 100% out of pocket and your future in academia becomes a little more uncertain.

Two days later, just as I had decided to use my own funds for the conference, I learned one of my colleagues had also gotten his paper approved.

"What will you do about the payment? It's a pretty big fee, not to mention the travel."

"The university is paying," he replied almost instantly. "Why wouldn't they?"

A funny feeling came over me. Every fiber in my body said something was off. *It's probably nothing,* I repeated to myself, almost like you would with a mantra until it becomes a reality, deep in your soul.

I completed my Ph.D. at the three-year mark. I felt happy, proud, and grateful to achieve this huge milestone. Once everything was said and done, I knew it was time to have a chat with my supervisor. I still had a few months left in my contract. But by law, the contract would end at the end of that academic year.

Despite the red flags, repeating my daily mantra had convinced me that asking for a contract extension was the thing to do. Nothing was wrong, after all, so why wouldn't I?

"I don't know," my supervisor said when I inquired. He had that same tone of voice that had sent chills down my spine many times before. "Why should I extend your contract? Why should I give you a tenured position?" he mused aloud. Naively thinking he expected a literal answer to his question, I quickly proceeded to explain all the reasons why. All the amazing results I had had in my research, how well I was doing teaching, other admin tasks I was involved in, the full package.

He smiled, listening, then said. "That's not what I mean. That's not what I'm looking for. Anyone can do research. You need to do more than that. And you don't. If you want to stay here, you need to help out more. Mop the floors in my office, that sort of thing. Do you understand what I'm saying?"

I did. And I didn't. My heart started beating so hard, its sound was ringing in my ears, deafening me to any external noise. More words followed. Some were more explicit than others. I was there. And I was not. I truly don't remember if I replied. If I did, it certainly wasn't anything powerful. The walls were closing in on me. It felt like the room was becoming smaller, and it was getting harder for me to breathe. All I knew was that I had to get out of there. But I didn't. I waited, stupidly, until he finally dismissed me.

"We'll see. There are a few more months left on your contract. We'll see if I'm convinced by you by the end of it. That would be all for now."

I smiled, stupidly, naively, thanked him for his time, and walked out.

During the following days, I thought a lot about whether I should tell someone about that conversation. As much as I wanted to believe my mantra—*it's probably nothing*—it didn't quite work this time.

I needed to get some things off my chest and voice the very real probability that I might not get a contract renewal, so I briefly told my family about it. But as I spoke, getting closer and closer to retelling my supervisor's words, shame took over. I simply couldn't. I had done that to myself. I hadn't been good enough. The way I'd been treated wasn't *that* bad. And it was my fault anyway. So I chose to say nothing other than the fact that my future at the university was uncertain. Responses varied, but all followed a similar theme.

"You need to work more."

"Was there some task you didn't do well? Or just didn't do? Pay more attention."

"You can't miss this opportunity."

I've always been my own worst critic, so whenever somebody suggested I was to blame, I, of course, believed it wholeheartedly. This time, it was no different.

I had a few months to make things right. And that was exactly what I planned to do. I did my best to be everywhere. To show people I was willing to do whatever it took. I worked harder. I kept longer hours. I may not have "mopped his floors," but I came as close as I could.

It wasn't long until my now former supervisor, current boss, found the perfect spot for me. A large conference was about to take place in our department. All my colleagues, both higher and lower on the "ladder" were part of the scientific committee. Me? No, I was not part of the scientific committee. I would be responsible for sitting out in the hallway, greeting participants, helping people find their names on a list, and handing them bags of goodies. Once that was done, I'd have to clean the hallway and other conference rooms.

At midday, another professor came around to see how everything was going. Seeing me at the check-in desk, he was visibly shocked.

"Laura, what are you doing here?"

"I'm responsible for greeting people. The Professor asked me to be here."

"But you're a staff member. This is a student's job. Each year we have students and volunteers at this stand. You should be with the other staff upstairs at the conference."

"Oh, it's fine," I replied. "It's nothing. The Professor probably couldn't find students in time and I was available."

"No, this is simply not right," he said, almost angry.

I knew he was right, but I didn't want to seem like an entitled little brat. So I kept my thoughts to myself, my head down, and assured him, yet again, that I was completely fine with the work I was doing. This was the first time someone truly pointed out something was off in my supervisor's behavior. And as much as all of it was starting to sink in, I was still caught trying to repeat and believe my mantra. *It's probably nothing.*

Not too long after that conference, I was chatting with a colleague when he casually said, "So, you might be getting promoted after all. You're getting your own course, right?"

"Sorry?" I said, unsure I had heard him correctly.

"The cybersecurity course they're introducing next year. That's yours, right?"

"I don't know anything about it. I didn't even know there was a new course, especially not on that topic."

"There is. Here, check out the proposal. It's on the website. I don't remember your thesis by heart, but the curriculum looks very similar."

As soon as I looked, I could feel my heart sinking. The curriculum was almost word for word the structure of my own Ph.D. thesis. My colleague was right. Logical thinking said this should be my course. But it wasn't. My name was nowhere on it. After a moment of silence, my colleague said, "You need to talk to him. To the Professor. There must be a mistake. Maybe he'll give you the lab first and then the entire course."

I knew I had to say something, but how?

Two days later, I stood outside his door, trying to master the courage to knock, rehearsing my speech in my head.

Breathe, I thought to myself. *You've got this. You've worked so much for this. Hours, days, weeks, months, years. All the effort you put in has gotten you here.*

Breathe, I told myself again. *You've got this. You can do this.*

Finally, I gathered all my courage, knocked on the door, and calmly entered. Looking him in the eye, I spoke my mind.

His response came swiftly and with no apology. "No, it won't be your course. You're not even doing the lab, you're not touching it. And I'm also not promoting you. As long as I'm here, you're not getting a promotion."

Sometimes, you have to learn to cut your losses.

Though the final moments were tough, I hadn't been stagnant during the course of the program, and new career paths opened up for me. I thought leaving would solve everything. But it didn't. Those years, those conversations, his words, his behavior, my naivety, all of that, it still haunts me.

When, years later, I finally told my mother a good part of the things he had said to me, she replied, with terror in her voice, "I didn't understand it was that bad. You should've told me. I didn't understand."

Did *I* understand? Partly. But I still clung to this idea that hard work must pay off somehow. No matter how evil, or corrupt, nobody can deny when you give it your all and do a good job.

By the time I realized how naïve these thoughts were, I had given so much energy to the work that I felt I had to cling to it for as long as I could. Anything less would be a massive failure that would be nobody's fault but my own.

I convinced myself to breathe through the hard times. To push through. Sometimes, though, the true strength is walking away. Leaving it all behind, no matter how big the loss. Taking those lessons, and maybe…just maybe… making something better.

Behind-the-Scenes

This is amazing! An essay collection with some of my favorite people on the planet, writing about topics I care about deeply! I can't wait to get started.

—

Wait…a book? Me? One of my essays in a…book? Like a published book? Is Kim serious? My essays can't possibly stand up next to what some of the others in the group will write.

—

What am I even going to write about? My stories aren't interesting enough. They're just boring tales of a misfit trying to find her way in the world and (usually) failing spectacularly. Who would want to read that?

—

OK. I guess we're doing this. I'm doing this. Let's start writing.

———

"Let's start writing." Easier said than done. I'll never finish this on time. Why do I even write? Why did I ever start writing? Why do I continue? Now that's a complicated answer.

———

I write because…

…the paper doesn't judge me. It doesn't interrupt and doesn't have an opinion on what I should say or how I should say it. It simply allows me to speak my mind and be myself.

…I can judge myself 100 times before anyone else can. And because I can be vulnerable. I can take the mask off and just be.

…when I choose to pretend, to become a character on paper, I do it consciously. I build that character the way I want to and because I want to and not to fit someone else's idea of me.

…writing is powerful. Because ideas and thoughts I didn't even know were there come to life in unexpected ways.

…it allows my emotions to come to life. Because I can feel things I wouldn't otherwise allow myself to feel. And at my most vulnerable, my writing protects me.

…I can build new worlds and make sense of old ones. Even though it can be brutally honest, my writing won't harm me. The paper is my friend, and it will listen to my thoughts, bringing sense and peace to where there's chaos and anger.

———

Sometimes writing feels so easy. I can get 1,000 words on paper with minimal effort. Other times, I stare at this computer screen for days and words just won't come.

Writing has always been my go-to. I write about the things that make me happy. And those that make me sad. The things I would like to be able to share with the world. And those I'd rather keep to myself. The moments I want to remember forever. And those I'd rather forget. Once everything is on the page, I find a new sense of calm. People might never know what I wrote. But I wrote it. It's no longer something bottled up within me. And maybe someday, someone will see my writing and feel a little less lonely.

Since I started sharing more personal essays, I have seen the impact words can make. And yet, here I am, still freezing in front of my monitor, scared to put this particular essay together. Will it have the impact I want? Or will it finally show the world I'm nothing but an imposter, and I have no place calling myself a writer?

Somehow, out of nowhere, there's this story on the page. It's a story I've been trying to write for years. I wanted to use my writing to process my feelings and the things that happened. Occasionally, I thought about sharing it, releasing it into the world to finally free myself from the burden of those events. But I couldn't. Each time I sat down to write, words wouldn't come out. When they did, they felt silly…like they could never do the story justice.

And here I am now, standing in front of this essay. Ready to share this story that I kept inside for years. Isn't it funny how "inspiration" works sometimes? A story brews within you for ages. You start it and delete it. Start again, delete again. You give up. Except you don't. It's always in the back of your mind, even when you're not aware of it. Until finally, one day, you're ready.

I've never felt so vulnerable and scared, and so strong and brave at the same time. Part of me can't help but wonder, is it any good? And what will people think? Whatever the answer…I'm at peace. This is my story. It's not something I wrote for the glory, the fame, or the virality. I didn't write it for revenge either, as some might suggest. I wrote it for myself. And for whomever else may need to read it. Anyone going through something difficult alone, doubting themselves, trying to convince themselves that "It's probably nothing."

I struggle a bit looking at it, wondering whether there

should be a more prominent conclusion. Something that screams, "Hey, look at me, this is the main point of this story." Perhaps it's the B2B content writer in me speaking, used to writing articles that always have some "key take-aways," or a "bottom line." Stories don't always have to have a conclusion, though, do they? It's a concept I've been trying to wrap my head around more and more.

The essay may be complete. But my story is not over. And whatever conclusions you get from it are yours, the reader. Each person is free to take with them what they need the most from the stories they read. That's the beauty of the written word.

Coming Out as Black

By Serine Goodmond

Abandon

"SHUT UP, YOU FUCKING N*GGER!"

One second earlier I was blackout drunk, mouthing off at a guy who'd disrespected my best friend. Then I heard the "ni—" and it was like I knew what was coming before my mind could catch up. My heart started racing. Blood pounding in my ears. Rage coursing through me. Suddenly, I was more awake than I had ever been in my life.

What the fuck did he just call me?

It was the first time (and only time since) someone said it to me like that: loud, to my face, and with venom. Looking back, I know the shock wasn't from just hearing the word. The horror was sharper because, the truth was, I didn't see myself in it. My dad was Black, my mom was white. I was "mixed."

*N*gger? Who? Not me.*

In that instant, I was in my body in a way I had never been before. This wasn't something happening around me; it was happening *to me*. I always experienced things separate from myself, living life like I was on the outside looking in. This was different. The details are blurry. Did anyone step in? Was anyone outraged? Or did no one know what to do with the one Black friend? Someone grabbed me, holding me back from exploding. Then came the sudden crack of gunshots. The guy I'd been screaming at was hit in the ankle by a stray bullet. The night fractured and whatever might have followed was swallowed by the chaos.

The memory of that night no longer belonged to me. It became about him. When everyone scattered, so did my memory. What had just happened to me, the word, the fire in my body, the brief clarity. I stumbled back into numbness, and the night blurred like a dream.

Willows is a tiny town in Northern California: deserted streets, tumbleweeds, rice fields under a punishing sun. After a jarring move, the Bay breeze was gone; I was landlocked and restless. Puberty only sharpened the confusion. My body changing, my mind grasping for definition, surrounded by whiteness. My proximity to Blackness was slim. Who was I supposed to become here? How could I make sense of myself?

The song "Mr. Wendal" by Arrested Development asks how we can call others uncivilized when our own society has brutally enslaved and killed innocent people. Those lyrics became the subject of a seventh-grade English paper of mine. While I didn't have the language for it yet, I felt the hypocrisy. How could a country call itself civilized while brutalizing and discarding its own people? How could violence against others be normalized and excused?

After 9/11, America's grief turned to suspicion, and

suspicion to open hatred. Classmates parroted what they heard at home: slurs against Muslims, "terrorist" tossed like a joke. I couldn't parse all the politics, but I knew it was wrong. That recognition, even unformed, pushed me further. With little around me to reflect my Blackness, I turned to media, music, books, films, photographs, piecing together what Sonya Renee Taylor would later name "the technology of being Black."* I became a student of Blackness, stitching identity from borrowed lyrics, scenes, and stories.

School became a kind of stage, debates and essays as performance, attempts to try *it* on, to validate the Blackness I wanted to claim. But by sophomore year, a new school and another move, the world around me pulled harder. The disruption of being new. The instinct to disappear. The desire to fit in. Torn between the comfort of acceptance and the discomfort of being different, somewhere along the way I abandoned the Blackness I was still figuring out how to claim. I learned it was easier to play along with the jokes and stay silent through the slurs. Drinking made that even easier, a way to blur the contradictions until the night my mouth ran faster than my fear, and I was reminded of the truth: you are not one of them.

Distraction

A sally port is a secure passage between two spaces. You enter through one gate, and it locks behind you before the

---

* Instagram: @sonyareneetaylor

other opens.

The first time I walked in one, the air felt heavy; my stomach knotted. Time slowed. To my left and right, 5,000 volts ran between twelve-foot fences crowned with razor wire. A guard watched from the tower as the gate clinked and rolled open. I stepped in, unaware it would become a passage I'd walk many times in the years to come.

This is real. I'm in a men's maximum-security prison.

A month earlier, I'd taken a non-violence workshop. Now I was here for the next one, deep in my study of the system's injustices, the repeated violence against Black lives. Reading was one thing; coming here was something else.

Like a time machine, that sally port would become a portal between who I had been and who I was becoming. Over the next three days, I moved through gates and checkpoints, circles in the gym, stories that stretched across lifetimes. Men who reminded me of my father, the same warmth, the same walls. On the final day, a question came, "How has violence affected your life?" I was unprepared for what would come.

Was mine a violent home?

Growing up, my dad was distant: wild mood swings, rarely affectionate and a presence that often made me hold my breath. After years of not seeing him, we finally connected during a visit, staying up late and talking in a way we never had before. For the first time, the resentment and fear I'd carried seemed to melt away. I began to understand him.

The next time I saw him, he had cancer. I didn't know it then, but that visit was my goodbye. A month later, I got the call. He was gone, without ever having said, "I love you."

This was its own kind of violence.

"How has violence affected your life?"

Everyone turned to me and, without warning, I broke down. My body shaking, the crying came hard and uncontrollable. I was taken over, gasping for air, unable to speak or explain what was happening. My dad had died five years earlier. Why was I falling apart now? I had never cried like this; I'd always kept it together. Everyone's eyes on me only made it worse.

Something cracked open that day, just as it had that night ten years earlier, and I was once again in my body. I wasn't just talking about my life; it was again happening to me. As the grief poured out, so did a strange aliveness.

For years after that first workshop, I made the two-hour drive once a month, sometimes twice. Long weekends, twelve-hour days in the prison, facilitating workshops, listening to and absorbing the stories of hundreds of men. Meanwhile, I was in school and working full-time, cramming my calendar with everything I thought I needed: big trips, festivals, and late nights.

Inside I felt different, almost at home. A version of myself I didn't yet know how to be anywhere else. Outside I was becoming distant and detached, an observer looking in. The exhaustion was wearing me down, but I didn't know how to stop. Only how to keep splitting myself in two.

Grief

The sun pressed down on my skin as I lay by the pool in the quiet of a warm midweek afternoon. For the first time in years, I was still. Just one day before, I'd been furloughed. At first came shame; why hadn't I been chosen to stay? Was I not good enough?

But there, under the sun, a slight breeze dissolved the fear into something else: relief. It was quiet. I had space to breathe, to rest, to be with myself. What worried me yesterday now revealed itself as a gift. The thing I'd been wishing for, handed to me on a silver platter, an impossible prayer answered.

Days slowed into rhythm. Sunrise soaks, long meditative hikes, pages turning by the pool, sweats in the sauna before bed. For once, I had nothing to chase—just time, quiet, and the strange luxury of being paid to rest while the world stood still. But there were cracks. Billionaires doubled their wealth while a virus engulfed the world. Some worked endlessly while others rested inside, me among them. Guilt and comfort knotted together. The hum began low and steady, something in me waiting to break.

Two years later, I would find a sealed envelope, a letter I'd written to myself during a workshop. Reading it felt like a message sent ahead, a clue of what was to come. I had penned my own prophecy.

I am unraveling.
I feel like a thread that was once really held together.
I was strong, reliable and had everything under control.
Over time the thread has slowly been coming undone.
All the fibers separating.
What was once so strong feels weak and wants to completely let go.
Is it time to go down the dark and long road of coming undone?
The hope lies in the next version.
I'll have to put myself back together in a different way.
This time I'll find a stronger weave, one that's more malleable, flexible and in turn will last longer.
The journey and process of unraveling.
To then begin anew.

The hum turned to a roar.

George Floyd was murdered in Minneapolis. On the same day, Christian Cooper was threatened by Amy Cooper in Central Park. Different men, same truth: white entitlement weaponized against Black lives.

Black Lives Matter.

I knew that, but now I could feel it. Rage came in a way I could never have imagined. This wasn't new; it had always been there, stitched into the fabric of my life, into every room where I'd swallowed discomfort to survive.

Who were all of *my* Amy Coopers, playing the victim

while terrorizing me?

Outrage consumed me. Scrolling. Reading. Typing. Reposting. I was not alone in my fury. Unhinged and bold. Feelings I felt before were being said out loud. No longer palatable. No longer quiet. Here grief was again. I was completely undone. I spun into mania, sleepless and raw. Memories I had buried surged back like flashes.

The confederate flag blanket from high school.

Not a single person asking if I was okay after losing my dad.

My car accident alone on the snowy mountain.

Racist jokes, tossed casually.

Thirty-one years of silence spiraling.

Pain as my fuel. My chest aching as my heart split in two. My body breaking. Weeping and wailing through this purge. I was dying and being reborn at once. In the depth of my pain, tears cleansed to clarity: my complicated relationship with my Black father; the violence done to Black people; the constant messages of inferiority. I had absorbed it all. Somewhere along the way, I had learned to feel shame for being Black. The connection was clear— this, too, was part of the violence: an attempt to make Black people hate themselves. I had been stuck in my delusion of safety.

Mixed. Fragmented. Surviving.

Not having slept in three days, I was grieving, unraveling, uncovering years of repressed pain. I started writing what would become *Dear White Friends*. Part manifesto, part confession. The first in a series of reflections, some shared publicly, others kept hidden.

Dear White Friends, I wrote. *I am crying so many tears right now. I have a habit of minimizing my experience, my pain, my fears, my worth, my excellence. Minimizing my Blackness.* The words spilled out of me faster than I could write. For the first time, I didn't soften the edge. I didn't dilute my anger to make it digestible. I spoke directly, and I meant every word.

It was clear the delusion of white supremacy* had not only shaped the world around me but also lived inside me. Poisoning me. Teaching me to shrink. To survive through silence. In my internalization of racism, I felt ashamed to identify as Black. So I chose the murky middle, the pretend safe ground.

But not any longer.

For years I had loudly protested Amazon, always explaining to friends that their exploitation was never worth the convenience. Over time it became a kind of joke, people rushing to explain themselves when an Amazon box was sitting on their doorstep or piled in a corner. "Sorry, Serine," they'd say with an uncomfortable half-laugh. There was something insidious in that ritual, their quick confessions meant to ease their own guilt, my righteousness meant to quiet mine. As if refusing one corporation could separate or absolve me from the violence I was already part of.

---

* I first heard this phrase from yogi Shirley Johnson.

As *Dear White Friends* poured out of me, I told this same story about Amazon, why I refused to buy from them, how their convenience was built on exploitation. But what I was really naming wasn't their violence, it was my own silence. The words were my stance. I would no longer let people forget I was Black. I would remind them, and myself, every day.

Unsurprisingly, and perfectly reflective of whiteness, most people missed the point. This wasn't about Amazon.

I was coming out as Black.

Shame

Shame is intended to make us feel wrong as a consequence of transgression. Sometimes it nudges us back toward integrity. But shame for what we cannot change is something else entirely. When the feeling attaches to our very being—to our race, our gender, the place we come from, it stops being corrective and becomes corrosive. The shame seeps in through the cracks, teaching us to find the corners where the light is dim enough to disappear. Over time it spreads, and we begin reading rooms instead of ourselves. The detachment becomes habit, then identity.

I came to understand that whiteness is less about white people and more about the institution of whiteness itself, a system upheld by a set of beliefs, a delusional ideology that white people are superior. White people have long been its agents, maintaining and reinforcing this power. But like anything that needs to sustain itself, its strength depends on numbers.

Whiteness rewards the smallest version of us, the agreeable, the adaptable, the compliant. It demands participation from everyone, attempting to shame those who aren't white and rewarding those who perform it. When I read Arlan Hamilton's words, "Having privilege, or being privileged, is not the problem. Entitlement is the problem," it clicked.* Whiteness perfected is a delusional superiority, fueled by entitlement, mistaking mediocrity for brilliance. Then comes assimilation, convincing, relentless, dressed up as belonging and masking as safety. Shame becomes both the tool and the weapon, assimilation its most seductive form of self-violence. Without realizing it, we get stuck in a performance, offering the illusion of belonging at the cost of self. And every once in a while, whether you decide or not, someone cuts the scene and they call you n*gger.

Acceptance

Telling the truth—especially the kind that implicates you—is both terrifying and liberating. I had to face how deeply I had internalized the violence I once condemned, to see how the same systems I resisted externally had taken root within me. I had to pull away and, in the quiet of my own mind, figure out who I really was.

I think back to the girl in middle school, uncomfortable as I stood up every morning to say the pledge of al-

---

* Hamilton, Arlan. (2022). *It's About Damn Time: How to turn being underestimated into your greatest advantage*. CELA.

legiance, disturbed by the hypocrisy. I'd long viewed the world through a particular lens: Black belonging to my father, to his side of the family, not to me. And because of my complicated relationship with him, I studied Blackness from the outside. Living in fragments, carrying pieces of myself I couldn't yet connect. I didn't know that silence would become habit, that disappearing would feel like safety.

All these years later, after many breaks along the way, I finally understand that despite my light skin, this is how I am seen. This is who I am.

What I was reaching for then was always me.

Behind-the-Scenes

I did not want to write this essay.

When the invitation came, I was honored. To be asked to contribute to this book, and to do so alongside writers who had ignited and solidified my love for writing. What a dream. I was excited at the chance to publish, to see my words bound and printed, to legitimize myself as a writer.

Or so I thought.

Then came my usual process: dragging my ass and putting it off. Convincing myself I could get it out quickly, then sitting down to write and stumbling through my words. Every attempt felt heavy, like trying to lift a story that didn't want to be moved. I had lived through it, but I was struggling to put the story into words.

I went through resistance, which, strangely yet unsurprisingly, mirrored the arc of my story itself: denial, shame, grief and acceptance.

• **Abandon**. More than once, I thought I had missed the deadline, maybe even on purpose, hoping it would disappear. A subtle form of self-sabotage, knowing we often sabotage what we care most deeply about. That realization alone told me I needed to stick this through.

• **Distraction**. I told myself I could choose another topic, something easier to hold. I busied myself with everything but writing. I had already written about this, hadn't I? In journal entries, half-finished essays, and Instagram captions that hinted at the truth without fully naming it. I didn't need to go back there. I had other work to be done.

• **Grief**. Rereading my old journals felt like reopening a wound. That year, 2020, broke something in me, and revisiting it forced me to look directly at the fracture; the confusion, the shame, the awakening. Some entries were so raw I could barely read them. I didn't want to relive the feeling.

• **Shame**. How embarrassing, I thought, to have to write an essay about coming out as Black. Would people ridicule me? Make it worse? The pull toward safety, the allure of staying in the shadows, was strong. But that resistance was the proof. If I were really past it, I wouldn't feel all this.

• **Acceptance.** When I finally surrendered, well beyond the eleventh hour, something shifted. I knew I had my story. The writing became an excavation, not of facts but of feelings. I revisited my notes from a writing workshop on layering. Remembering how to braid narrative, memory, and reflection so that the story breathes. That technique became my way through.

I wrote in the early mornings and late at night, stealing hours around my long workdays. Each session was both exhausting and clarifying. I caught myself trying to neaten the story, to make it linear and digestible. But that's not how my story goes. I had to let the essay live. It's not a perfect piece. It's a living one. It breathes, trembles, re-members. It carries both my fear and my freedom, then and now.

Fear of how others would read it: white readers who might treat it as a confession rather than a declaration, Black readers who might question the legitimacy of my experience, people who knew me then who might feel implicated. Clearly, I was still feeling not Black enough. I had to keep reminding myself I was writing for me, and for anyone who has ever fractured themselves to survive.

Somewhere in the writing, I stopped performing clarity and started practicing honesty. This was a kind of coming out, another layer of integration, another release. I allowed the mess, the contradictions, the questions that still don't have answers. In revisiting what I tried so hard to forget, I found something I didn't know I'd lost: tenderness for my own becoming. I let the essay reflect not just what I know, but where I am now, including the part I'm still learning—how to be this version of myself in the light. It's gotten comfortable in the room by myself, the light turned up bright. There are still places where I feel timid in being fully me. Writing this essay is one act of coming back into that light.

I didn't want to write this essay. But at every turn, it became clearer: I needed to.

The Whispers

By Kim Marsh

"Your dad was Christian, right?"

"Yeah, Protestant."

"So, I'm just wondering…why did you choose Judaism?"

The words seem strange to my ears. There is no real answer to this question because the very premise of this question doesn't make sense. The confusion envelops me.

I pause and notice the blood rush to my cheeks. I feel called out, but I don't know for what. After all, to say "choose" implies there were multiple options, and that's not exactly what happened here.

But, I do understand what's behind this question.

Here are the facts: I grew up with a Protestant father and a Jewish mother. I celebrated, culturally, both Christian and Jewish holidays. I did not attend church or temple. I did not receive communion, nor was I bat mitzvah'd. I felt super grateful that no set of beliefs had ever been imposed upon me. I identified as an atheist for a brief period in high school before learning the term agnostic, the label I then used for years followed by the (now seemingly pretentious) phrase "spiritual but not religious."

Let's call it what it is: I didn't believe in G-d, and I

thought this made me better than other people.

I've always considered myself an open-minded person who prides themselves on creating spaces of inclusion and belonging. But somehow, religion quietly became a third rail. When it came to discussing this aspect of anyone's identity, I was respectful, but absolutely judgmental. I lacked curiosity and compassion, the cynicism and critiques too loud in my own head.

I didn't understand how a belief system was something that could be passed down to you. It felt akin to saying "I believe unicorns are real because my mom said so." I judged people who felt they needed to go to a building to speak to some higher power. I internally cringed when anything veered into the realm of some "big man in the sky." People who quoted Scripture made me uncomfortable. I eschewed the seemingly contradictory nature of religious institutions; on the one hand preaching love for all and on the other excluding and denigrating so many. On the rare occasions I needed to step foot inside a house of worship for a wedding or celebratory event, I felt completely self-conscious and out of place.

So, the logic behind the question of why I chose Judaism wasn't sound; it assumed the false premise that I chose to become more religious and that picking *which* religion followed after said choice. It didn't happen that way at all. That's what feels so easy to know and so hard to explain.

Still, I'll try.

"Well, it's a few factors," I begin to respond. "But also," I immediately hedge, "I have some reservations. Because I'm conscious that there will be some people who will say that the only reason I've reclaimed my identity as a Jew is because I want to weaponize it. That I'm only now saying I'm Jewish so I can say I'm a 'Jew for Palestinian liberation.'"

And, not-so-deep beneath the surface, I wonder if there's some degree of accuracy to this statement. It scares me and makes me feel like a fraud. To be clear, it's not the conscious intention behind it. But the crux of my recent awakening *did* begin in October 2023.* This is when, amidst Palestinian suffering and genocide, I learned what the term "Anti-Zionist Jew" meant. Seeing images of *Never Again Means Never Again for Anyone* struck a deep, deep chord in me. There was rising shame for neglecting this part of my identity for so long. There was a feeling of both connection and disconnection, like a once thick rope that had been whittled down to a single thread, tenderly, and almost invisibly, bridging me with the Jewish people I saw in these photos, Instagram reels, and news articles. There was a familiarity. A deep sense of kinship.

A thought—"these are my people"—found its way to my brain, followed almost immediately by another: "No, they're not." The feeling of connection evaporated as quickly as it arrived.

---

* To be clear, this conflict and occupation began years before October 2023, and it does not end with a ceasefire.

"And it's not just that," I say. "There's other things, too. Like everything with my great-grandmother."

I then tell the story of my great-grandmother, Leah Vascovitz. How I'd learned just recently from my mom's cousin all about her story. How she had been persecuted for her Jewish identity, and how she narrowly escaped from Moldova with her young children—including my grandfather—in tow. And how, with this new picture developing before my eyes, I began to notice the existence of that thread again, once invisible, now glowing brighter and brighter for my attention.

None of this happened all at once, but in uneven steps over the last couple of years.

My spiritual journey, my life journey, the history unfolding around me, and messages from my ancestors have led me here. (Heavy, no?)

Seeds along the way have been planted. Then neglected. Then planted again. Then watered. Whispers in my ear, guiding me gently in this direction. To keep nurturing this garden and not let it go.

But how to capture all of that? How do I find the entrance to the path?

It started with a knowing.

Then I think it continued with Jewish Voice for Peace and their daily action calls.

It evolved to Rosh Chodesh (new moon) practices. An exploration of Jewish mysticism.

It moved to classes and communities (including one I eventually left because they wouldn't denounce Israel's crimes against humanity).

But then I got to the Torah. I just didn't get it. Couldn't figure out the bigger picture. It felt overwhelming, like I'd missed the chance. If I hadn't learned all of this as a kid, it's probably too late.

But the thread…it still wouldn't break.

So I turned to research.

A flicker of understanding with the Talmud. Interpretations of the Torah.

A Google search: "Pro-Palestinian synagogues near me."

Zero results.

Temporary defeat.

A drifting; a sense of untethering.

A chance conversation about a story from the Quran.

A reminder of the thread.

A deep knowing: *I want to explore the Torah again.*

Another search. "Anti-Zionist synagogues. Virtual."

A few results.

A few clicks.

A heart swelling.

Many tears.

And now here I am. Sitting in front of my computer, attending virtual Shabbat, singing in Hebrew (terribly). With people who center Palestinian stories in Torah study. With people who lead services on Friday and march outside ICE detention centers on Saturday. With people who say things like "we are seeking atonement for non-vigilance over the rise of fascism" in their Yom Kippur prayers. To pray for the first time in my life, and to do it so radically, is a gift I didn't know I could even want, but is one I deeply needed.

A thought occurs to me: maybe this has been about community and belonging this whole damn time. But it had to be the right (for me) community, and it had to be true (for me) belonging. I have come to believe that it is hard to find a feeling more powerful than the feeling of being fully seen, fully known and fully loved.

As my exploration continues, I feel my great-grandmother, and all who came before me. I even feel my dad. They are all here with me, their hands at my back. The month of Elul in the Hebrew calendar (when I began this essay) signifies a sense of returning. And I feel that so deeply in this moment. I am turning, and I am returning. To myself. To that whittled down rope that one day, long ago, in a past that existed possibly before I even came into my own consciousness, connected me so tightly to something. That tether that hasn't quite let go of me yet.

I could let my shame, my guilt, slice down on the thread with one final chop, severing me from all of this forever. Or, I can listen to the whisper telling me it's time. The whisper telling me to start weaving something new together. To fortify it. Telling me maybe there's a way to become closer, stronger. I can look over my shoulder, and I can anxiously ask "what if?" and wonder. Or, I can listen to the whisper and grab hold of this a little tighter.

I've decided to listen to the whisper.

Behind-the-Scenes

I put off writing my essay until days before publication.

Well, this particular one.

My original essay was drafted nearly two years ago when I conceived of this project and immediately, resolutely decided to write about my dad. It was obvious. His death was, after all, the one topic I'd been avoiding for years. (Not just in my writing but in my life; the two went hand-in-hand. "I've never fully grieved," became the throwaway one-liner I'd share with each new therapist.)

But then, in September of 2025, I was doing some reflecting after the question of "choosing" and began crafting a piece I thought I might post on Substack. As I grew more honest and more raw with every keystroke, a thought began bubbling up: *Can I actually publish this? It's so nuanced, and it feels like there's too many opportunities to be misunderstood.* And then another thought: *Oh, shit, I think* this *is supposed to be your essay for the anthology.* Unfortunately, as the editor of this anthology, I had the benefit of making such a last-minute change. And I did.

It's here that I want to cover my burning need to be understood with a nice cozy blanket, telling it "shh, shh, it's going to be okay; you're not needed anymore," but she had way too much caffeine and is wielding a nasty red pen.

It's here that I want to acknowledge that I wonder how my friends who have suffered from spiritual abuse might experience my words; I know of the religious institutions that have caused violence and harm to many, and I understand the toxic environments that many spiritual and religious communities breed.

It's here that I want to remind you, and myself, that the essay I would have written about this topic at age 18 is vastly different from the one I am writing today. Which leads me to believe the one I might write in twenty years (or next week…) has the possibility to be completely different from this one.

But none of that makes this any less of my truth. It doesn't make it any less real.

And, oh, this is hard for me! Because I'm the caveats-on-caveats-on-caveats person. I mean, this is a "thing" for me. I need to give statements context. I want to explain myself. Every email I send should come with a TL;DR accompaniment. I write dissertation-length diatribes of my feelings. I'm the person who texts you 10 minutes after we hung out to say, "This is what I meant when I said such-and-such by the way." I just need you to know how I feel and what I think and all the nuance that might be at play.

So the thought of something being in a complete package, printed on actual paper and out in the world without the ability to make tweaks or edits or add prologues or footnotes or afterwords or amendments is essentially my worst nightmare. I want to explain all the feelings and all the questions I still have and what I mean by the words "religion" and "spiritual" and "community" and "belief" and "G-d."

And…and…and…

But this essay was not the place for those explanations. This essay needed to end. And with its ending, the release of control. Control over how you as the reader interpret it. Control over what you think of me. As a writer. As a person.

Many of the things that held me back from wanting to publish this essay are precisely the things that threatened to hold me back from following the whispers.

So much noise. Fear, shame, my inner critic, self-doubt, that running ticker tape. But I'll keep trying to get quiet enough to hear what's meant for me.

The Things That Change
(and the Things That Don't)

By Therese Temitayo

Behind-the-Scenes

THE STORY I'M GOING TO TELL YOU IS FUCKING EMBARRASSING. It involves a lot of anxiety, a poorly drawn penis, and a breakdown. I'm not sure what you're supposed to learn from it.

Maybe it's a cautionary tale about procrastination, or a story about my ego being my saving grace and my downfall at the same time. Or maybe there's nothing to learn, and this is just an odd recounting of my medical history and its real-world consequences. Maybe I need to be talking to a therapist and not writing to an audience.

Lucky for you all, good therapists are hard to find. Pens are not.

I knew I was meant to tell stories at a young age. I don't know what drew me to it, but as soon as I could pick up a pencil, I refused to put it down. I was six, writing about witches and potions, and then I was eight, writing about alien invasions. Writing was an endless amusement park with no lines, and I was obsessed. I was twelve when I took my first creative writing class in middle school, and it sealed the deal for me—I wanted to become a writer, no matter what.

Suddenly, I was writing about student spies and dangerous monsters—with structure! There was imagining and planning and plot rollercoasters. I was in my glory. I embraced my flair for dramatics on and off the page at the expense of my (fantastic) teacher who had the patience of a saint. There were times I burst out laughing in the middle of her class at something I wrote; it often got to the point where I was laughing so hard, I had to leave the classroom and take a walk. I loved every second.

Our final assignment for the class was to write a five-page story about whatever we wanted. My teacher was incredible—she pushed me to do so much with my stories, igniting my creativity to the max. With a glamorous level of delirium, I stayed up all night working and ended the story with twenty-six pages. Bless her heart, my teacher loved it. It was the first story I ever got a "100" on. Not only was she so incredibly proud of me, but I was also so proud of myself. From that point on, I was known as the writer of my grade, the girl who wrote a novel for a five-page project. It was everything I'd ever imagined on paper, and everything I wanted for myself. For me, telling stories was the most fun a person could have. I knew I wanted to write not just for my career, but forever.

Then I entered high school.

In my defense, I was still riding on my wins from middle school. I had just gotten a brand-new laptop, I had done so much writing—lots of character building—over the summer and finished most of my summer reading homework. I felt so ready. Alas, I was not.

My high school was aggressively difficult, to say the least. The very first paper I wrote was for my English class, and I could swear up and down it was great. I was ready to get my first A+ out of many. Imagine my shock when I got it back with a big fat "65" at the top. This shocked me; I was sad, and I was angry. Offended, even. My freshly fourteen-year-old brain couldn't process it. *I'm a writer! I don't deserve a 65! What does my teacher even know about writing?!* I honestly thought it was just a fluke—*I just have to get used to high school writing.* But things got progressively worse, fast.

It was essays on top of essays on top of projects and films and math and chemistry on top of more essays. I tried my best to keep up with everything, but when it came to writing papers, I struggled the most. I would stare at the screen from morning until night and write nothing. It was confusing and uncomfortable—my amusement park suddenly had height requirements I couldn't reach. Awake in the wee hours of the morning, all alone, I'd try to string together any words that made sense. But I'd come up with absolutely nothing.

I was devastated. At fourteen, I had an identity crisis: I was a writer who couldn't write for shit. Yet I refused to admit it. I was angry at the world, at my teachers, at everything. I wondered if maybe it was because my projects were boring—I wasn't writing fiction, I was writing about Daisy and the champagne in *The Great Gatsby*; there's nothing fun about that. But when the rare opportunity to write fiction presented itself, I still found it difficult. Humiliation began to take over.

I find it odd recognizing and accepting that feeling: humiliation. It's how I feel right now writing this story. I can't believe I'm writing something about myself that my family is going to read. It makes me feel sick. And at the same time, I feel nostalgic about it. I'm sharing these things that affected me, and how I moved through them, grew from them. These issues that felt insurmountable are memories now. Humiliation must be my proof of life—how humbling.

I had never been so stressed. At this point, my already competitive school was throwing academic expectations at me faster than I could react. Once I reached 10th grade, the pressure of SAT prep *plus* my lackluster grades started weighing heavily on me. On top of that, I didn't know who I was anymore. How could I be a writer that couldn't write? I was beyond overwhelmed. I was scared.

My emotional state was detrimental enough that my parents took notice, so they took me to the doctor where I was diagnosed with severe anxiety and depression. Now, this was back in 2015. Though my parents aren't like this anymore, back then they didn't "believe" in diagnoses like that. They pushed me to do my absolute best and expected the best, regardless of how I felt. To them, this diagnosis was just a distraction. It went unacknowledged and was nothing more than a confirmation for me that no matter what I did to try and be better, the only thing holding me back was *me*. And now my parents were aware and monitoring me tenfold. I felt like I'd snitched on myself. My amusement park now included child locks and surveillance cameras.

My ego couldn't take being watched like a baby, so I acted like everything was fine. When my parents asked me how school was, I lied and said it was going better. I started doing whatever I could to pass my classes: I was cheating on tests when possible, cutting corners in my group projects, begging my teachers for extensions. I even went as far as plagiarizing my papers so I wouldn't have to stare at stupid blank pages anymore. I remember feeling relief receiving one of those papers back, a B+ at the top of the page, only to feel my heart sink because I didn't recognize a single word on the page as my own.

The pressure was suffocating, and I didn't have any confidence in myself to do better. I started skipping classes out of fear, opting to cry my eyes out in the bathroom or telling the nurse I was feeling ill so I could go home early. If my parents asked about my early dismissal, I lied and said I had a free period or my club was canceled. This happened every day for months. I was spiraling, and I didn't know how to handle it.

Luckily for me, I had a great teacher on my side. My 10th grade English teacher had faith in me from the moment I stepped into her class. She had read my writing and knew I was capable of so much, so when I started to fall behind, she required I attend her office hours to catch up on all the work I was missing. And when she found out I was falling behind in *all* my classes, she made sure I was going to *everyone's* office hours. She would walk me from room to room, making sure each teacher knew I was there and needed help. I hated it, and yet I held onto her for dear life. As much as I wanted to sink into myself and disappear, she kept me afloat.

Still, my ego held me back from embracing all of the changes I needed to make to pass, and my improvements were moving at a snail's pace. My lack of progress made me bitter and envious of my classmates. Even worse, I was becoming jaded towards school and towards writing. I was tired of not being good enough even though I was trying so hard. I was tired of being so stressed out at school and taking it out on my family at home. I was tired of feeling like writing papers was a waste of time. I felt like I was walking through a sandstorm with no sense, reason, or purpose. I physically couldn't bring myself to do anything anymore.

My teacher refused to give up on me, and she quickly realized that my spiraling wasn't normal. She also realized something was physically wrong before I did. In a meeting with my parents, she told them to take me to a specialist.

They did, and soon after that I was diagnosed with Grave's disease, also known as hyperthyroidism.

Looking back at it, the signs were all there: my hair was falling out in clumps, I couldn't sleep, I was eating but couldn't gain any weight, and my resting heart rate was over 240bpm. My doctor's jaw dropped when she first saw it, like she was surprised I was still standing.

I was put on medication for my blood pressure and for my thyroid, and I had to take all sorts of vitamins to help with my low energy. It was bi-weekly blood draws and a ton of check-ups with the doctor, but I was genuinely recovering, albeit slowly. It took me a long time to finish my papers and projects, but I was doing the work in a way that worked for me. That typically looked like waiting until that post-medication burst of inspiration hit to finish my work—which just happened to be a day or two before my assignments were due.

It was not a perfect method, but I was writing my own words with my own hands again. I was blessed with understanding teachers who gave me and my situation a lot of grace and didn't mind giving me extensions when needed. I went from nearly failing out of high school to graduating with a B average. It felt like the writer in me had woken up from a coma, and I had truly survived. I graduated high school, got into college, even got a bit of scholarship money, and was on medication that helped. Things were changing for me, and I wanted to see what would come next.

In 2018, I arrived at college where I was functioning truly on my own for the first time. I loved my first semester. I decided to major in Creative Writing and Cinema, and things were better than good. I was adjusting to my medication, enjoying my own company, making my own money with my new on-campus job, and—hold your applause—I was doing really well in school. I was a revamped writer with a revamped process: stagger the classes and wait until the last minute to write the papers. "Last minute" was where I knew my best work would come out. I wrote a paper for my English 102 class 30 minutes before I had to turn it in and submitted it unedited.

Not only did my teacher love it, but he also encouraged me to submit it to a competition on campus.

I did. And I won.

I wrote an opinion essay for a different class the night it was due and submitted it at 11:59 p.m. on the dot.

It was later published in the local newspaper in my college town.

My ego was inflated. Philosophy, English, Marketing, Language. You name it, I could write about it—and *I did*. I felt like the person I was in high school (who couldn't write a paper to save her life) never existed. *I was never a bad writer,* I thought, *I just write better medicated! And under pressure! It's not that I don't understand it, I just can't do my best work without a time crunch.* I convinced myself that this process was what made me a writer. This pressure was the missing key that I needed this whole time. And no one could convince me I was wrong because it was working, and pretty damn well.

Until it wasn't.

Sophomore year in college, I took a screenwriting class, and our only project was to write a script about whatever we wanted. That was it. We had the entire semester to complete it. We didn't have any other assignments, and we could use our class time to do it as well. There was no way we couldn't get it done. But believe me when I say, I absolutely found a way.

The structure I had been using up until this point was this: get assignment, read over assignment, wait until the day before it was due, start in the morning, finish before 11:59 that night. But with this sort of assignment? This structure left too much room for me to work with.

During class, instead of writing the script, I worked on

assignments due for my other classes. I caught up on papers I had missed or gotten extensions on. And I worked like this right up until finals week, by which time I had exactly three pages of this script written. I spent most of finals week catching up on papers and projects that I hadn't finished throughout the semester, and by the time I finished with those, it was the day before winter break, and I had a couple hours to turn in my script.

I was running on about four hours of sleep, and I had never consumed so much coffee in a day. But my ego was the size of a hot air balloon. I really believed I would get it done. I'd done it before, and I could do it again—and better!—because *I was a writer*. I could write this script with my eyes closed.

By some miracle, even with my eyes open, I managed to write a total of fourteen pages. Unfortunately for me, the page requirement was ninety. Needless to say, I failed that class. My teacher didn't even review my paper. Just took one look at the fourteen-page document and gave me a big, glorious zero.

I know I shouldn't have been shocked, but I was. I was devastated. I sobbed my eyes out alone in my dorm kitchen. Selfishly, I was furious that my teacher didn't even read it, as if the paper I had worked so hard on wasn't even worth looking at. My ego refused to admit that it really *wasn't* worth looking at. The pressure had caught up to me, and I was no diamond to turn into—I simply got crushed. It was the first and only class I ever failed in college, and it destroyed the confidence I had in my ability to write good work once again.

To make matters worse, Covid hit the semester after, forcing me to be isolated with my assignments *and* my thoughts. It was the worst I've felt in a long time, and the most doubt I ever had about myself as a writer. My junior year was spent in quarantine, and I took the least amount of classes possible to release a bit of pressure. Still, none of my assignments were turned in on time. There was a new sense of panic that lingered through the passing of every deadline. Like that was going to be it. My professor would read it and hate it, and everyone who read my work would just hate it. I began to question if I even wanted to be a writer at all.

When I finally graduated in 2021, I wanted to be excited, but all I felt was a strange, stinging numbness. Almost two months after graduating, my laptop broke. I couldn't get a new one and was forced to use my mother's old computer. It felt like a sign for me: just stop while you can. I didn't know what I wanted to do anymore; the writing system that I had put in place for school had not only failed but was now the only system I had to rely on to carry me through. I was 21, I didn't even know how to "life" yet. All I knew how to do was fail.

I was scared. At the same time, I was angry and over-confident. I felt like my world would burn up if I wrote one more bad piece, yet my ego refused to admit there was anything wrong with my writing. I was a *published author* for crying out loud. And I held on to that part of me, regardless of how painful it was. This back and forth pushed me into a very dark period. Stuck, I didn't write anything for months.

In May of 2022, I was mindlessly scrolling through TikTok, and I came across a journal entry prompt.

"Do you feel like you have any missed opportunities in love?"

It felt like such a silly question. I'm pretty sure I rolled my eyes at the time, because why was TikTok interrogating me about my failed relationships? I was barely 22. How many opportunities at love could I have possibly missed? But for some reason, I felt a pull to answer. So, almost on a whim, I grabbed a pen and began to do something I hadn't done in more than five months—I wrote.

Without expectation, without pressure, I wrote how I felt. I wrote about my experiences, I wrote about my pain. I wrote about everything. I didn't think about grammar or spelling or punctuation or making it sound a certain way. I just wrote for myself. And when I finished, I felt so good.

The next day, I did another journal entry. And another the day after that. I wouldn't go as far as to say I was repairing my writing self-esteem, but it felt like I could acknowledge the shattered pieces around me instead of ignoring their presence, and that felt good. To really see a part of me and become comfortable with it made me feel better than I had felt in ages. Though I was scared, I wanted to write. I wanted to get back into it with the love I had when I was younger.

In June of 2022, I decided to sign up for a virtual writing group and found a public event hosted by The Open Book Company (led by this anthology's editor, Kim). I remember feeling so nervous but so excited to be getting back into it. I was gonna go in, broken pieces and all, and still be a writer. I was gonna write something, not finish it, and then talk about it and have the world not blow up. And I was going to be surrounded by people who understood that process.

Unfortunately, things quickly took a turn for the worst. There's no way to delicately say this, so I'll put it bluntly. Soon after I logged onto the Zoom call, a troll assumed my name and began drawing penises on the screen. Yes, that's right. Someone decided to make a mockery of our event, renaming themselves to randomly match that of other joiners and causing chaos by drawing obscene images on the presentation. Of course, since the offender had my name, I was kicked out of the call.

Looking back on it now, all I can think is that this whole situation really was so fucking stupid. It was such a random thing to happen, though it felt so dire in the moment. I'm laughing at the thought as I write these words, because it's so damn ridiculous. Childish, annoying even. I keep thinking this is something that would have happened on a sitcom or something.

Booted out of my first connection back to writing in ages, I sat on my bed, the Zoom window closed, staring at my mother's ugly Superman screensaver. I was heartbroken.

It was one thing to get kicked out of the call, but for something I didn't do? The person I had become didn't matter. The writer that I wanted to be? Forget it. Before I knew it, I was in the midst of a panic attack. I was ready to give up entirely. It felt like I had fucked up before I even got my foot in the door. I didn't want to be near my computer. And yet, my one comfort was still writing. So, through my snot and tears, I wrote. I wrote about the shame I felt, the embarrassment, the anger, the sadness. I journaled about the disappointment at finally getting the courage to show up as a writer again and how this might have been a sign I wasn't worthy of a writing community, a place with people who might have felt the same as me.

And at that very moment, I got a notification from the host of the writing circle, Kim. She had been told what had transpired during the call and was very apologetic about the situation. My first initial thought was to let it go.

Just tell her it was okay, and then never join another one of those writing circles, or another writing group, ever again. But as I stared at the screen of my computer, I felt the exhaustion hit me. I was tired of hiding. I wanted to be honest. I wanted to feel seen and by a fellow writer who might truly understand me. So I told this complete stranger the truth. I wrote to her about how the situation really triggered me, and that I wasn't sure if I would be okay in such an open space if it meant experiencing anything like that again. To my surprise, Kim was so understanding and so kind about it all. And I cried again.

It was such a simple act, yet I felt so seen and comforted. And it was my writing that did that. It feels a little silly to say this because, in reality, we just shared a simple, honest conversation, but I truly felt like I spoke through my writing that day. I had shared with someone one of my broken pieces, and the world didn't explode. Because of what I wrote, I was able to become closer with another person. Through all my turmoil, I was still a writer, and this experience changed what that word meant for me.

So, what happened after that fateful conversation? I was empowered. I went to the next writing circle. And the next one, and the next one. It's now three years later, and I'm still a member of The Open Book Writing Community, still going to the writing circles.

I'm still writing.

I wouldn't say that my anxieties around writing have healed completely; I'm working on that. But I'm sitting here, at 11:34 p.m., months after I was supposed to turn this story in (sorry, Kim!) and I'm feeling good. The panic I found in my chest in moments like these has dulled to a small beat. The stress I used to experience all at once now comes in controllable waves. Because no matter what happens, I know now for a fact that I am a writer, regardless of deadlines or due dates. Writing is my biggest pain, and yet my biggest joy.

I was recently prompted to think about how I wanted to feel at the end of writing this story. My initial response was that I want to feel like a weight is off me, I want to feel relieved. But I remembered that I wrote a long time ago that I don't want to feel relieved writing stories anymore, as if it's a chore or an assignment I need to get off my plate. I want to feel proud. Like I made something worth being proud of.

When I was struggling as a teen, I didn't know what kind of writer I wanted to be. Truthfully, I still don't. All I do know is that I'm a writer. A good one—with severe anxiety, and that's okay. I don't work well with schedules, and that's okay. I do things late, and that's okay(ish). Sometimes I don't even finish (but I *did* finish this one!). And that's okay. As long as I'm writing, I'm a writer, and that won't change.

Curious if I'm Anxious?
Take a Look at My Nails

By Katie Boateng

ON DECEMBER 4, 2014, I WOKE UP AND GOT READY FOR MY DAY as an Undergraduate Enrollment Counselor at the College of Western Idaho. I commuted daily from Boise to Nampa, about a 30-minute drive, depending on the traffic. I can't remember the details of that morning, but I imagine it began like most days for me: I would have showered, dressed, and put on makeup while I drank my coffee. I probably left for work early like I always did to make sure I was there and ready to start my day by 8:00 a.m. I do remember that it was a rainy morning, and there was heavy traffic.

Underneath the sound of the raindrops and click of the windshield wipers, I was likely listening to NPR or a podcast while paying attention to the cars around me and going slower than usual due to the weather. I would've probably seen lanes of cars on either side of me, as there are four lanes on that interstate in the section I was driving. I have acquired anosmia (no sense of smell) due to an upper respiratory infection I had in 2009, so I couldn't tell you what my car smelled like; however, I imagine that it smelled like the "new car smell" air freshener that I habitually hung in my vehicles.

Here's what I do know: About 15 minutes into the

commute, I was hit by a semi-truck that didn't see me and changed lanes too early. My maroon Saturn spun across three lanes of traffic and smashed against the inside guardrail. It felt like I was both spinning forever and for no time at all. I remember thinking to myself, "Is this really happening?" Once I hit the guardrail, I remember asking myself, "Did that really just happen?" I simply sat there, stunned. Luckily, I hadn't been hit by any other cars as I traversed the length of the highway, and I wasn't *physically* injured. When I was hit by the semi-truck, I instinctively took my hands off the wheel and let the car spin of its own accord. If I had tried to hang onto the wheel, I imagine that the car would have flipped over, so thank goodness for small mercies and instinct.

I don't remember how long I sat there before the police arrived. I do remember thinking that I was annoyed that not one vehicle stopped to check on me. They all kept driving as if my life had not forever changed in an instant.

Once the police arrived, I was interviewed by an officer who took a look at me. I wasn't hurt, so they didn't call an ambulance or make me go to the hospital. The officer took my statement and my insurance information and exchanged it with the driver of the semi-truck who hadn't been able to pull over for half a mile because of the traffic. (I never interacted with the driver myself.) The officer took a quick look under the car, confirming the axle on the car had snapped and I was unable to drive it. He called a tow truck to pick up my car, and I was released to leave.

The police officer hadn't required me to be checked out by paramedics. I figured that since I wasn't physically hurt, I should just go to work. *After all, he said I'm fine, so I must be fine,* I thought to myself.

There are different forms of trauma. I wasn't physically injured but—I would later realize—I had been emotionally traumatized by what had happened. However, at that moment, I took my lead from those around me. *She's okay, she's not hurt, she's good to go,* I kept hearing.

So why did I feel a sense of immense panic in my chest?

My husband, Stephen, came to pick me up and took me to work. When I arrived at the office later than usual due to the accident, I shared with my coworkers what had happened and they sympathized with me. *Oh no! We're glad you're okay! Terrible about your car!* Then, we all moved on. Later that day, one coworker commented to another that I had "had a little fender bender" and that's why I came in late. I was slightly irritated, but it made sense; he thought it *was* just a little fender bender. Otherwise, why would I be there? Everything was fine.

What's the Next Step?
When I reflect on this experience, what sticks out to me most is the nonchalance with which I handled almost being killed on my morning commute. I was hit by a semi-truck, spun across three lanes of traffic, narrowly missed oncoming vehicles, smashed my car into a guardrail which snapped the car's axle, and I decided that I should still just

go to work, business as usual. I didn't process any of the emotions of this experience. I didn't take the time to say, *Holy fuck. I almost died and that was scary.* This was, in hindsight, unsurprising. My coping mechanism in any emergency or emotional situation is typically to be very level-headed and then move right along.

As a child, I learned from my parents that crying and emotions were okay, "But what are you going to do about them?" In other words, "Okay, you're sad right now or your feelings are hurt, but what's the next step?" This question became almost a mantra and, to this day, whenever something negative or critical happens in my life I immediately, almost automatically, ask myself, "What's the next step?" I have a difficult time just feeling my feelings.

Sure, I was upset that I got hit by a semi-truck, but what is the purpose of sobbing or being scared about it? Is that productive? Does that help with anything on a practical level? With this perspective-taking snap back to reality, I quit crying or being emotional, and I moved forward.

Two weeks after my car accident, I flew from Boise, Idaho to Valdosta, Georgia to attend my sister's graduate school graduation ceremony. I had my first full-fledged panic attack on that flight. I was with my mom, Reysan, and my brother, Jonathan. Though I don't remember the actual flight itself, what I can remember distinctly is the terror of knowing (not thinking or worrying, but *knowing*) that I was going to die. I had never had a panic attack before, so I didn't understand at the time what was actually happening to me. I learned after the fact that there was some turbulence on the flight. I believe the turbulence is what triggered the panic, and that the unprocessed trauma from the car accident decided to come out to find me. My mom and I have since talked about this experience. Given my complete lack of recollection, she recounted my behavior. Apparently, I couldn't control my breathing or heart rate, and I dug my fingernails deeply into her arm. I also have zero memory of the return flight back from Valdosta to Boise. My brain has blocked both out, likely because they were too scary for me to process. I knew I had no control of anything going wrong on either flight, just like I had no control over a semi-truck almost killing me on my way to work.

Since that trip, I have struggled with flying for fear of triggering another panic attack. (It may be a self-fulfilling prophecy at this point.) I have flown; however, candidly, I don't remember most of the flights that I've taken since 2014. I believe I enter into a dissociative state because my brain and body simply can't handle it.

I flew to England in 2016 to celebrate the Christmas holiday with my sister, Marie, who was stationed in Spain at the time. After the visit, we all flew back together to Spain to my sister's home, and I got very drunk on the plane because I was so worried about the flight. Spain is very liberal with their alcohol on flights policy and you're able to purchase mini bottles to take on board with you. My sister-in-law, Mel, kindly told me that I probably didn't need to open my fourth mini bottle of red wine because we were going to start the descent soon. My shame rising, that was an eye-opening moment for me, and I decided I needed to find other ways to cope with flight anxiety.

To alleviate my stress and help me combat my concerns about a panic attack, I started to take Xanax when I flew. I took a flight in 2019 from New Jersey to Idaho to visit my family. On my way home, I was so scared about the flight that I took a good deal of Xanax. Stephen picked me up from the airport after I arrived back in New Jersey, and we talked the entire way home from the airport, about an hour's drive or more. A couple of days later, he referenced something we spoke about and I was surprised. I was completely certain that part of the conversation never took place; he assured me it had.

Physical Manifestations

My parents announced they were going to separate when I was 13. This news completely shocked me. They started to argue in front of us, something they hadn't previously done, and I was really worried about things going wrong in my family. I didn't have any control of the situation, so I coped by reading a lot and chewing my nails whenever I felt anxious. Around this time, I began to pick at the cuticles on my fingers and toes. Since then, I have periodically chewed my nails and picked my cuticles to the point of making them bleed or causing an infection from an ingrown nail.

I now can use my nail status as an indicator of my current level of stress. If I'm picking my nails or toes a lot then I know that I've got a lot of stress happening and that I need to take a pause, focus on myself and my body, and make a plan to reduce that stress. For me, this is usually in the form of more walking or doing yoga. I have trouble with processing and feeling my emotions because I typically don't see the value in "just feeling" things. *Okay, I'm overwhelmed or sad or anxious, but also, I have a lot of things to do, so let's just move on.*

In addition to the nail chewing and picking, I know that my unprocessed trauma and emotional disconnection manifests itself in my body in other ways. At some point after the car accident, I started to grind my teeth in my sleep. Officially, this is known as bruxism. Stephen told me that I started making loud smacking sounds throughout the night, and I would often wake up with pain in my jaw and sometimes a headache. I spoke to a dentist about it, and she checked my back teeth. They were already substantially ground down. I would need to wear a specialized nightguard to prevent exacerbating the situation.

The grinding could be related to stress, she said, and to reduce my stress if possible. She emphasized that if I didn't wear the nightguard and continued to grind down my teeth that it would lead to worn-down or broken teeth, increasing my sensitivity and possibly leading to loss of my teeth. (The teeth grinding hasn't stopped, and it has contributed to gum recession. I have a prescription toothpaste that I use to help with the gum sensitivity. If it doesn't help in the long term, I may have to get crowns on the affected teeth.)

In January 2023, my family moved from Budd Lake, New Jersey to Cypress, Texas. Stephen was offered a new position within his company, and his primary role was located in downtown Houston. We had just purchased our first home in New Jersey in November 2021, so moving across the country a short 15 months later was not something we had anticipated.

When we moved to Cypress, we decided to keep our New Jersey property and rent it out. It took far longer than we expected to find a tenant. We didn't end up securing one until April. During that four month period, I was working part-time and Stephen was working full-time, both of us from home. We had our two-year-old son, Kwame, at home with us because we were paying for our mortgage in New Jersey *and* our rent in Texas. Paying for childcare was out of the question.

In early April 2023, Stephen pointed out that I had something "going on" underneath my left eye and asked me what it was. I disregarded it. A few weeks later, while on the phone with my mom, I noticed I had a weird, white-looking patch of skin on my right hand. I have fair skin with many freckles and moles, so I've regularly seen a dermatologist my entire adult life for skin checkups. My mom advised me to make an appointment as soon as possible.

When I went to see the dermatologist, they looked at the different discolored splotches on my body and shined a UV light on my skin to see if the discolored spots were fluorescent. They were, which meant I had something called vitiligo. I didn't know what having vitiligo meant or would mean for the rest of my life, but I immediately began crying at the news. The doctor told me it was an autoimmune disorder that can be triggered by severe stress. Moving unexpectedly from New Jersey to Texas with a toddler in tow, no childcare, trying to work from a new place while attempting to secure a tenant as we covered two mortgages…stressful? I suppose that all qualified. To say nothing of the unprocessed stress built up from years of anxiety. It all conspired together, coming out in the form of an autoimmune disease. My vitiligo was my body's plea for me to stop and pay attention to myself, to stop and realize how stressed I was, and to see that I couldn't keep doing all of the things I was doing anymore.

Well, if rest was the answer, I quickly realized I wouldn't get it in the form of sleeping. At least, not deep sleep. The recommended amount of deep sleep is 20-25% a night, or roughly 1-2 hours. My six months deep sleep average is 29 minutes per night, or 5%. I typically wake up for 45-90 minutes a night depending on how stressed I'm feeling in the daytime. I'm unable to fall asleep without listening to a podcast or an audiobook. My therapist pointed out to me that this may be because I need something to distract my anxious brain from overthinking when it's time to go to bed. She wondered why; so did I. I used to be able to sleep without needing an audiobook or podcast, so when did that start?

Oh. After my car accident in 2014.

Processing and Moving Forward

How do you go back and process unprocessed trauma? Candidly, I haven't figured it out yet, but I'm trying. As a start, my therapist asked me to sit still for 15 minutes a day. During that time, I'm not allowed to do anything else. I can't read or listen to a podcast, watch TV or scroll on my phone. I'm supposed to just sit and be still. So far, this has been excruciating for me to do. (Recently, I made it for seven minutes before I got up and started defrosting chicken for dinner.) Another thing she's asked me to try and do is to be okay with my emotions. When I cry, I am just supposed to cry. I find this extremely difficult. I'm uncomfortable sitting with my feelings, and I want any strong expression of emotion to be over and done with as quickly as possible.

I have been exploring EMDR (Eye Movement Desensitization and Reprocessing) therapy with my current therapist but haven't done many sessions. According to the American Psychological Association, EMDR is "a structured therapy that encourages the patient to briefly focus on the trauma memory while simultaneously experiencing bilateral stimulation (typically eye movements), which is associated with a reduction in the vividness and emotion associated with the trauma memories." To do this effectively, you need to be able to remember the traumatic event, and—try as I might—I simply can't remember the flight that triggered all of my flight anxiety.

At the time of this writing, it's the end of January 2024, and I have a trip to Fort Myers, Florida scheduled in mid-April. I already have daily thoughts with concerns about the flight. What if the plane panel flies off and I get sucked out of the plane to my death? Will that moment be as terrifying as I imagine, or will I feel vindicated knowing that all of my worrying about what could go wrong was valid?

In the meantime, this is my truth. I hold unprocessed trauma and anxiety in my body, and it has manifested itself in different ways including teeth grinding, vitiligo, and unrelenting anxiety. I will continue to go to therapy, to read all the self-help books, and to try to improve myself over time. I think of anxiety as an annoying friend. They think they're there to help me and they probably have in the past. But I'm ready for new coping skills and new friends.

Behind-the-Scenes

I started therapy back in 2010, four years before the accident, because I became an acquired anosmic in 2009. I lost my sense of smell due to an upper respiratory infection during my first year of college. Having anosmia made me very anxious because I felt untethered from the world. I describe it as existing in black and white or as if there's a clear plastic bubble between yourself and everything around you. You're still seeing everything but there's a barrier that you can't quite penetrate to fully enjoy the world. Why am I bringing this up? Because I don't want to make it seem that I was a non-anxious person prior to my accident. I was anxious even as a kid. I was anxious because of my anosmia. And then the car accident was the cherry on top of the anxiety ice cream.

I've always had an anxious temperament. The car accident didn't cause me to become an anxious person; I already was one. However, the car accident solidified for me the way that I cope with things. It allowed me to realize that I am a chronically anxious person. My mind is powerful and wants to protect me. I appreciate this, but now

I need to work on feeling my feelings and dealing with my emotions so that I can move forward with my life in a healthier way.

As for that planned flight in April 2024 to Fort Myers, it never happened. I found out that I was pregnant in January and that we were having twins in February. The morning of departure, I was panicking before I even left the house; my heart rate was in the 130s just putting on my makeup. I knew when I started to cry that I didn't want to go. I was so worried that my panicking would harm the babies somehow and I just couldn't make myself do it. I also missed trips to Washington, DC and Costa Rica later that year because of flight anxiety. In every instance, I felt a completely overwhelming sense of shame for not being able to "just go" on the plane.

I'm overall an extremely logical person which is hilarious because anxiety isn't logical. If I simply could tell myself "Don't be anxious" and it worked, then my life would be great. There's a quote floating around that by worrying you're suffering twice, and it's such an annoying quote to me. I KNOW that I don't need to be anxious, but I can't help it.

In terms of writing this essay, I definitely feel a sense of imposter syndrome any time that I write anything, because I don't view myself as a writer. Why would someone want to read what I have to say? Why would they care? Will this really help anyone else? Although I ask myself these things,

I know in the back of my mind that what I have to say can potentially help someone else know that they're not alone.

I haven't shared a lot of this information publicly. It has taken me a long time to get these thoughts down on paper, and it does make me uncomfortable to be so vulnerable and so open about my personal struggles. What if people judge me? However, the simple act of writing this has helped me reflect on my own anxiety and seek new tools to help me feel less anxious. Ultimately, I've decided that what I have to say is important because it's therapeutic *to me*.

To Open or Not to Open
Our Marriage: That Was the Question

By Nicki Pappas

"I'm afraid I'm going to have an affair," I said, a bit of soft pleading in my voice.

I looked over at my husband of thirteen years. He sat next to me on our dark gray couch. His eyes seemed to indicate he wasn't taking me too seriously. "Just don't," he replied.

———

The notion of "infidelity" conjures many feelings in me, and likely in you, too. As a society, particularly in the United States, we publicly declare we value monogamy, while many people privately live non-monogamous lives. Often, we judge "unfaithful" partners as immoral, as if marital fidelity is the greatest indicator of morality. We may discount people's positive attributes and contributions to society and reduce them to this one act. As unfortunate as this is, I understand why we do it. At least in part, we employ this binary defense mechanism because *we* would never want to be betrayed in this way. And that's what infidelity can feel like in a closed relationship: betrayal.

I got married at the age of twenty. Coming out of a chaotic and abusive home environment, I longed for connection, protection, and stability. Stephen, the man I married, was all those things for me and more. For a solid decade, we followed a deeply codependent script for our relationship. In an effort to win his approval, I altered aspects of my personality to become more like the person I thought he wanted me to be. By denying, repressing, and suppressing my own needs, I assumed my "low-maintenance" demeanor made me more desirable. I believed embodying his "dream girl" would mean he wouldn't abandon me. Then one day, I had a revelation: I'd abandoned myself.

Through years of Internal Family Systems therapy, I befriended the parts of me I'd previously exiled. As I began to uncover who I truly was, I realized that I liked that person. By consistently showing up for my inner child, I started to trust myself. This led to me establishing a secure attachment to myself, an attachment that was no longer dependent on Stephen. As I became more comfortable with my full humanity, I became a healthier human. Stephen and I had a healthier relationship. I felt such joy and excitement at the prospect of growing old with him. I thought I had everything I ever needed. I was content.

Until I wasn't.

My discontentment ramped up when I encountered a man I'll call Darren. We met through artistic endeavors. From the beginning, he was a huge advocate for my writing. His words of encouragement addressed a wound

I'd developed in childhood and carried for decades. The message I'd internalized was that I wasn't creative, clever, or compelling enough for anyone to listen to me. On numerous occasions, Darren contradicted that messaging by saying I was "prolific." He told me he was honored to be asked to read my work and that my writing "was visualizable." He even told me once, "I don't tell you these things because I think you need to hear them. I tell you because I believe them."

And I believed *him*.

Early in our friendship, Darren did a huge favor for me. Though he helped me on that particular day because he was a good friend, there was also a palpable chemistry between us. We flirted while we were together, and we continued via text messages afterwards. Even though I'm a naturally playful person, I'd not actively flirted with someone since getting married. The butterflies fluttering from my stomach to my chest caught me completely off guard. That night, I was still reeling as I closed my eyes to find some sleep. As my head turned back and forth on the pillow, I realized something with a jolting shock: I had a major crush on another man.

The next day, a dear friend brought me tea and sat on the bed with me while I cried. Between sobs, I confessed to her that I was afraid I was about to blow up my marriage for no good reason. I'd already come out as queer to Stephen on New Year's Day 2022. Before that, I was the one who pushed us to leave a church where I'd been spiritually abused, leading to an exchange of many of my core religious beliefs. I was such a different person from the twenty-year-old who said "I do" in 2010. Would my desire for an open marriage to explore other relationships be the final straw and push Stephen away? That's right. Have I mentioned I wanted an open marriage? And it wasn't simply because of that one flirtatious day with Darren. I'd been spending a lot of time thinking about this.

The first time I tested the waters around the topic of non-monogamy, it was purely out of curiosity. Someone I personally knew was in an open relationship, so I asked Stephen one night as we were getting into bed if he'd ever be open to an open marriage. The silence in the air was loud. When I inquired if he wanted to know my thoughts, he said, "I assume you want one or you wouldn't be asking." My reply that night was, "I don't know. I'm not sure if I'd ever be comfortable with someone else seeing me naked." (My stomach and other areas of my body are covered with stretch marks. The vulnerability required to be naked with someone else is scary.) He responded, "Only if it came to that." Calmly, I assured him it *would*, in fact, come to that. I'm a very sexual being. I mean, I wasn't thinking about the possibility of an open marriage so I could simply sit on park benches sipping coffee with people I'm attracted to!

Darren's presence brought the subject of non-monogamy back to the forefront for me as my feelings for him intensified. Soon after my tear-soaked conversation with my friend, I told Stephen I had a crush on Darren, though

I didn't disclose the depth of my desire. While on one of our evening walks, I broached the non-monogamy conversation for a second time. Though I wasn't threatening an ultimatum, I expressed to Stephen that I didn't want things to continue as they were. He was confused about what was lacking in our relationship. He interpreted my ache for an open marriage as evidence of a deficiency in himself, saying, "If you were getting everything you needed from me, you wouldn't be looking for it elsewhere."

Struggling to explain myself, I tried my best to help him understand that it's too much pressure to put on one person to be everything to and for another person. It's not fair for me to look to him to fulfill my every want and need, and I don't want him looking to me for that either. With measured breaths, I attempted to assure him that there was nothing wrong with the person he is. My longing to open our marriage was an authentic example of, "It's not you. It's me."

Our wires further crossed when Stephen admitted he couldn't wrap his mind around how I could say my love for him wouldn't be diminished if I pursued another romantic relationship. Thinking I had the perfect response to this common misconception, I brought up how the birth of our second and third kids didn't minimize our love for our firstborn. After all, love isn't a finite resource. Then, I recounted a scene from *Kung Fu Panda 3* that I believed perfectly summarized what I was saying. In the movie, the main character, a panda named Po, reunites with his birth father. At first, Po's adoptive father is jealous, until he tells Po's birth father, "Having you in Po's life doesn't mean less for me. It means more for Po." I just knew this tear-jerker would be the clincher that helped seal Stephen's understanding of where I was coming from.

I was wrong.

Obviously, I was left with no other option than to rant. Launching into a tirade about the confines of monogamy within a patriarchal society that uses marriage to control women, I got all my frustrations off my chest. I felt better, but we didn't come to a consensus that night about next steps. Honestly, I felt a bit defeated and ready to just live out the rest of my days in monogamous marital bliss, or as close to bliss as I could get. Imagine my shock, and subsequent delight, when we attended an outdoor vendor market one sunny summer afternoon a few weeks later and Stephen purchased two books about non-monogamy.

Reading *Polysecure: Attachment, Trauma and Consensual Nonmonogamy* by Jessica Fern* unlocked insights into my psyche. Fern wrote about how some people are non-monogamous by choice of lifestyle while others are non-monogamous by orientation. As I read and reread that some people are non-monogamous as an orientation, I felt known in a way I never had before. Realizing that I simply *am* non-monogamous brought clarity to my entire life.

For most of my marriage, I'd been nervous I would

---

* Fern, Jessica. *Polysecure: Attachment, Trauma and Consensual Nonmonogamy*. Thorntree Press, 2020.

have an affair. I cut myself off from friendships with men to ensure I wouldn't cheat on Stephen. The anxiety about my own potential infidelity stemmed from prior relationships I'd ruined by cheating on some of my boyfriends. I'd been shamed into believing something was wrong with me for wanting to date multiple people at one time. In thinking the issue was non-monogamy itself (in these contexts, often referred to as "two-timing"), I shunned this part of myself. In actuality, the issue was in how I had previously practiced it as a teenager—without my boyfriends' knowledge. At the age of thirty-three, I was learning I could practice ethical, or consensual, non-monogamy.

I don't regret the time I spent in a monogamous marriage. I think I needed monogamy for a time in order to heal and to stop the harmful patterns I'd been repeating. In many ways, monogamy served as a coping mechanism that provided parameters for me. However, in the wise words of Emmy Kegler, "Coping mechanisms that served me well, even saved me, five years ago may suffocate me now."* That essential period of practicing monogamy also taught me that not every urge can, or even should, be acted upon. Granted, I experienced great repression as a result and needed to continue tending to the wounds that accompanied this. But I was becoming better equipped to spot the differences between self-control and self-suppression.

The relief I felt about having language for my experi-

---

* Kegler, Emmy. *All Who Are Weary: Easing the Burden on the Walk with Mental Illness.* Broadleaf Books, an Imprint of 1517 Media, 2021.

ences after reading Fern's book cannot be overstated. Naming my orientation as non-monogamous brought additional levels of self-awareness. But how would Stephen react to this news? The night I decided to tell him, my heart was pounding. My voice was shaking. My pits were sweaty as we sat on the back patio. With the outdoor lights twinkling above us, I came out a second time to Stephen. This time as non-monogamous. I explained to him that I felt desperate to have an open marriage, not because he was insufficient as a partner, but because this is who I am. Who I have always been.

I was able to let Stephen know that I want us to be able to celebrate one another's growth. I want us to be able to communicate gratitude to one another for what we've gained as a result of our relationship. Then, we can cheer the other person on to pursue freedom, individuality, and autonomy. Because of the secure attachment I've established with myself, I've nestled into accepting that things are as they should be. Not in a spiritual-bypassy-way, but in an inner-peace-way.

Stephen didn't get on board that night and—real talk—there was a bit of resentment inside me, as I felt like I was stifling a part of myself while awaiting his response. I'd come so far sexually in advocating for myself and my needs, like when I told Stephen I wanted a vibrator for our anniversary in 2023. I celebrate the journey thus far and also know that there's still so much farther I want to go. Sometimes, I begrudge that my exploration of non-monogamy hinges on someone else. Sure, I *could* say, "Fuck his feelings. I'm going to explore sex with someone else whether he's OK with it or not," but I'm not going to.

So, what am I supposed to do with this knowledge of my non-monogamous orientation? How beneficial can it be to embrace a non-monogamous nature while simultaneously navigating limitations imposed by my current partnership? Well, I don't know what's next in my marriage, but I know the kind of person I want to be as I traverse this new terrain. This includes seeking to understand rather than bulldozing over Stephen in an effort to be understood. It also includes a lot of engaging with the intention of maintaining connection more than engaging to be right. If I enter a conversation with Stephen just to be right, I may "win" the argument or discussion, but it's not worth what I lose in the process. No matter what, I want to live in alignment with the things I value most: curiosity, authenticity, and vulnerability.

I'm no longer afraid I'm going to have an affair. The energy I put toward worrying about infidelity and about what people would think of me is better spent focused on getting to know myself. I accept the person I am, and my opinion of me matters the most. Therefore, I will move forward fully showing up in spaces as a vibrant, queer, ENM woman, telling *my* truth and *the* truth without shame, and relentlessly pulling the threads of self-discovery.

Behind-the-Scenes

"What will people I know think of me?" This is the question I played on repeat when working on my essay about non-monogamy. My essay wasn't a detached analysis about the topic. It was about my identity as someone who is non-monogamous. For people to reject this part of me would feel like them rejecting *me*, because my non-monogamy is such an important part of who I am.

While trying to decide what to disclose, wondering how people I know personally would view me after reading the essay influenced me far more than I wish it would have. More specifically, I was consumed with worry about those from my evangelical days thinking negatively about me. Back when I was an evangelical Christian, I would often pontificate about the "sanctity" of marriage. Would those from my former life think I had completely discarded any belief in marriage being "holy" or "sacred"? Would they see me as an inconsistent hypocrite?

But also, why did I care so much about what people thought? Especially people who were no longer active participants in my day-to-day existence. Well, that stems from my image consciousness. There's a ton of stigma around non-monogamy in evangelicalism (and yes, outside of it, too). Here I was worried about being labeled a hypocrite by a group of people who practice hypocrisy religiously. They say they value lifetime heterosexual monogamy but then practice infidelity at rates similar to the rest of humanity. This is not me judging people for having affairs. I'm simply calling attention to the fact that this supposed "sin" is being practiced by the very people who have classified this action as such.

My marriage is still very sacred to me. That's why I've been so cautious and thoughtful in my conversations with my husband. Also, I reserve the right to change my mind. Always. Whether that be because of new external information or new internal messages. I'm not a hypocrite. I'm a fucking human. And I love being human and embracing my ever-evolving humanity. I love and accept myself. So, it really doesn't ultimately matter if "they" do. Whoever this elusive "they" is.

On top of navigating big picture questions behind-the-scenes while writing my essay, I was also dealing with shifts in my personal life. A friend sent me a Ted Talk video of Esther Perel talking about infidelity. Watching that made me come to terms with the reality that I was having an affair, even though nothing was "happening." This was because Esther Perel defines an affair as having "three key elements: a secretive relationship…an emotional connection…and a sexual alchemy."*

---

* Perel, Esther. (2015, March). *Rethinking infidelity…a talk for anyone who has ever loved* [Video]. Ted Conferences.

All three of those components were present in my connection with Darren to varying degrees. I began to question if I wanted to stay married. I told Stepen I wanted a divorce because I was feeling like marriage was a whole scam in a patriarchal system. At the same time, I was grappling with an egoic transformation, a death and rebirth of a part of myself that was helping me believe the best about people and trust them when the opposite had been true for so long. This wasn't because I was naive but rather because I liked how I felt when I believed the best about people, unless they demonstrated otherwise.

When I scheduled a one-on-one call with Kim to discuss my essay more specifically, I told her I was struggling with "owning" my non-monogamy. To own it, I felt like I needed to be at peace internally. Kim asked if I was, and my honest answer was no. We then explored what the disconnect meant for me.

At one point, I said, "I may never have an open marriage, and I'm okay with that." When I said that, I meant it. Later, I changed my mind. It became, "I may never have an open marriage, and I'm very much *not* okay with that." Now, I'm back to the former mindset, and I worry that people will think I'm wishy-washy and unstable.

When I sit with and look closely at this fear, it ultimately begins to dissipate. I know that the people whose opinions matter most to me allow ample room for my full humanity.

Inheritance

By Jinx Malcolm

Discovery

"THIS IS QUITE ABNORMAL," THE THERAPIST TOLD ME AS SHE monitored my heart rate.

Afternoon sunlight streamed through the slats of the blinds, landing on soft, dark blue decor. It was like any other therapist's office with a desk, comfortable couch, and a few chairs. I was 22 when I sat in one of those chairs with clips on my ear lobes. I was looking at her screen to my left.

"What do you mean?" I asked. "This is how I always feel. This is normal, what do you mean?" Panic roiled in my stomach, and my face went hot with red flush. The word "abnormal" echoed down the dark cave of my mind.

"Well, a resting heart rate is between 65-95 BPM, and you are at 120 BPM just sitting here." A little relief settled in as I realized I hadn't actually done something wrong. "Whenever we talk about your dad, your heart rate sky-rockets." She stood and crossed the room to get a book. As she handed me the book, she covered a section of it with a sticky note. I read the information below it:

Grandiose sense of self and feeling of never doing wrong
A lack of empathy
Seems to take enjoyment from others' pain

I honestly cannot remember the rest. What I do remember is a feeling that I had gotten him discovered, and now I was in big trouble. "Does this describe your dad?" she asked, as if she had all the answers right there in that small manual. I agreed that it definitely sounded like how he acted. Though I did recall bouts of him crying, I didn't know how he felt about himself. She removed the sticky note to reveal the title of the section: Narcissistic Personality Disorder.

I couldn't really comprehend what she was trying to communicate through what seemed to me to be a dramatic display. She diagnosed me with Major Depressive Disorder and referred me out for "further assessment." I was referred to a psychologist, a friend of hers from her university back in Wisconsin. I thought I had my answer: It had been me and my depression the whole time. It was my problem, my fault, and now my responsibility to fix it. As if "fixing" depression was so easy.

Learning

My father found out he was having me at age 19, and I was born when he was 20. My mom, 25 at the time, came as a package deal; my half-sister was just two years old. After my parents had me, it was not long before they became pregnant with my brother. By 22, my father had three young children, a high school education, and (apparently) Narcissistic Personality Disorder. With this and a genius intellect, he landed a government job developing software for the stealth bombers of the 90s. He began to make a lot of money off of bombing innocents and could finally afford his version of "the good life." Even with this, there never seemed to be enough money to clothe his children or pay half of their health insurance. He could buy a brand-new sports car for racing, but I was only allowed to wear my sister's hand-me-downs. (As a non-binary and genderfluid person, I loved dresses, but mostly I wanted to match my best friend and brother in their Yu-Gi-Oh and Pokémon shirts with zip off cargo pants.)

Not only that, but his behavior meant my mom was basically enslaved to him, having to provide food, clothing and education to three children all by herself. All this while he smoked a pack a day, partied with his music scene buddies, and bought expensive sound equipment. Unbeknownst to me, I was as sheltered as you could be without full-blown living in a monastery or commune. Things could only be a certain way or you'd get grabbed, scolded, or humiliated; however, the rules were subject to change at any time in any circumstances for any reason. This kind of logic, especially as a kid—a neurodivergent kid who connects everything—is incredibly confusing. You are presented with reality in a vacuum.

Punishments in my house ranged from the normal (like grounding) to the completely abnormal. They could include "push your face into this wall until your nose bleeds or you cry." Or, if there was a spill, he would grab our heads and shove our faces into the carpet, saying "lick it up." We would have to lick the carpet until he was satisfied. Experiences like these are one of the many reasons I have large gaps in my memory.

Words matter and have power. They shape reality and the world around you, as if real magic. In this environment, it is easy for a child to internalize the anger, the fear, and the words, "You were a mistake. I wish I had never had you." When you hear that your life was a mistake over and over again, especially as the brain develops, it becomes who you are. It's the kind of internalization that turns into vitriolic self-hatred.

He demanded respect from his family. Because of this, I began to address him by "Sir" and used formal language to communicate that I respected him. This only drove his anger, as he thought that my usage of these terms meant I thought he was old. This, apparently, was a sin against his very humanity, or so it seemed from the way his face clouded over, and his eyes pierced through that storm, as if to strike me down where I stood. What I didn't understand until much later is that he used the word "respect" when what he meant was "fear" and "unwavering loyalty." No matter what language I used, how gentle my verbiage and intent, my words were constantly met with backlash. At some point, I even used words as a weapon to fight back, slinging accusations and profanity. This played right into his mind games, and I received even worse backlash. It felt like I could never do or say the right thing. I now refer to him in conversation only by his given name. This is an act of distance as well as defiance.

Before seeing my new therapist, I decided to disown my father. For so long, I naively hoped he would change, despite the abuse. Recognizing his sadism and trauma enabled me to finally cut him off so I could live. It was 2014, and my brother had just been hospitalized for a suicide attempt. Even in the hospital, he would not leave my brother alone, chastising him and talking down to him.

It was the last straw.

Loss

While disowning him was liberating, the damage was done—his words shaped my identity, the very structures of my brain, and instilled persistent self-loathing. I just knew there was something wrong with me. After all, his words told me every day that there was something wrong with me. This belief laid the shaky foundation for adulthood that I am still dismantling piece by piece.

For years, I was unable to develop deep relationships with healthy people. I cheated on the first person I ever romantically loved. I couldn't hold a job. I graduated college but was so burned out that the very idea of getting a job made me want to die. So, I decided to try the referred therapist who "specialized" in trauma. Within a few sessions, she diagnosed me with complex post-traumatic stress disorder (C-PTSD) and mentioned with surprise that I was one question away from a Dissociative Identity Disorder (DID) diagnosis. She explained that "regular" PTSD can be treated pretty easily with eye movement desensitization and rehabilitation (EMDR). Adding in the word "complex," though, meant that I had sustained multiple traumatic events over time and who knows how long it would take to treat all that, if it was treatable at all. I couldn't believe I was getting this diagnosis just three months before graduating college—with a degree in psychology of all things and a minor in cognitive science. (I should have seen it coming!)

Some people seek therapy because they feel they have lost themselves. I feel as though I never had a self to lose. Well, maybe the homophobic, racist, misogynist puppet my parents created within me. A self they constructed of shit-smeared paper mâché, complete with strings they programmed and plucked. I went to therapy to cut those strings. I went to therapy because I had an out of body experience where I watched as I cheated on a man I loved. That therapist had me take a short quiz, then blamed everything on bipolar disorder. I went to the therapist who mentioned NPD because I had a panic attack when I sliced some cheese for a sandwich. I went to the new therapist to feel loved, seen, believed and held. And hopefully to stop having panic attacks over cheese.

None of this meant that I was incapable of feeling loss. Regardless of the daily abuse, I thought I had a dad who loved me and, if it came down to it, would protect me from others. I believed I had a mother who would do the same. I had a little brother who I thought was my best friend. I had an older sister that I wanted to be like when I grew up. They were no longer laidback and fun-loving as I had perceived them as a child. They turned into angry, vengeful, petty people who took small pieces of each other to consume. Presenting themselves as happy, quirky, and loving to the world, behind closed doors, they took off their facades and showed their true colors. Humans only change if they themselves desire and value change. It is comfortable to cling to past cycles and behaviors, even when abusive, as sick as it sounds. My family appeared, to me, more interested in comfort over growth.

People try to comfort me by saying my parents did the best they could in the situation and that they are sure my parents love me underneath it all. Not only is this not a comfort, indeed it is harmful to every ounce of anger I have earned. These words enforce every punishment inflicted, every humiliation endured. Furthermore, can you love someone you refuse to understand, do not accept, and, in fact, outright reject? If my parents loved me, why did they want me to fear them? If my parents loved me, why did they say they would kick me out if I was queer? That is not love.

I left him behind with the more complex abuser, my mother. For a long time, I thought it was me and her against the world. Not so. While I worked and went to college full-time, she partied. When I needed her to help me untangle the mess of what happened to us, she went to the bar. She was needed, and she did not show up. The pressure of the loneliness compounded and collapsed in on itself like a dying star. It felt like holding that black hole inside my chest. It opened me, stretched me across its vast and endless corona, across space and time. No one talks about the loneliness of being fooled into thinking there is a loving and happy relationship with one's own mother, only to discover that she is abusive, toxic, and does not, in fact, have the capacity to love her child, or at least not the queer scapegoat.

This loneliness leaves a nagging emptiness. Never quiet, it is whistling wind across the crater of my heart. Sometimes the noise of other emotions can muffle the sound, if only for a moment. But the emptiness persists. It is behind every thought, every breath, and every choice I make.

It is so clear and easy to leave the blatantly abusive parent. The parent who put his hands all over, the parent who created a war zone with his words and games. It is much easier to see the transgressions, the choices of evil. Some people say there are no evil people, only bad choices. This makes me scoff with cynicism.

Expansion

After many years of therapy with the trauma therapist I was referred to, who emulated my mother, both in toxic positivity and in gaslighting, the pandemic began. I fired her. I lost my best friend, a dog named Mimi, that very week. Soon after, I ended up losing the rest of my human friends to white supremacist bootlicking. Unfortunately, the cult of capitalism and white supremacy had me so fooled that the lockdown was the only thing that made me stop hustling and really examine my life. Even though I figured out that I am a non-binary genderfluid person in September of 2019, I still felt there was something I missed. I had heard I "was a mistake" for so long that I didn't know anything else. There remained this underlying feeling of *I am wrong. My being is wrong.*

At 30 years old, three years into the pandemic, after a cycle of hiring and firing a couple more therapists, I was diagnosed with ADHD. I finally had the language to describe many of my experiences with reality, which led me to read all the books I could about neurodivergence. This exploration revealed the many behavioral and internal issues I have had my whole life that landed outside of ADHD and into traits of autism and OCD.

Ever since I figured out that I am developmentally, fundamentally different from most people, I have found so much space to forgive myself. The wound of *what is wrong with me?* is finally beginning to heal. The start of the pandemic was a forced pause that saved my brain from breaking all the way. I was burning out so fast. *Everyone else can work a part-time job and come home without being exhausted. Not me.* I assumed I was a failure for not managing my own trauma, my own C-PTSD.

And, one day, a realization appeared: it was all connected. All of this hustle and mental self-abuse to keep up with everyone else was because I inherited such poisonous language about myself. If I never stopped, I would have kept going and going and going and going until it would have literally killed me.

Community

As I began to find myself, I started seeking people who would challenge me to grow, while holding a space of compassion and acceptance. I was seeking my chosen family. Every night, I whispered a prayer to myself and anyone who might be listening. Surely, there are people out there who want to disrupt these systems of abuse. These systems are all connected. I scoured my local library for resources. I read and read and read. I searched my local community for people who had similar beliefs; beliefs that people are not property, that people are meant for so much more than work and war; beliefs of life's inherent value. I was searching, desperately, for anyone who could pass "The Human Test." After coming up dry in my local ventures, I discovered that where I grew up is considered a piece of the Bible Belt, encouraging cycles of abuse and poverty. I wasn't going to find like-minded people where I live. So, I began to seek community online. First, I found the Ill Witches, a group of disabled folks who centered women and non-binary disabled voices. Then, I found the writers, who held even more magic. I felt like my prayers were getting answered.

Gaining community outside this restrictive region allowed me to open my eyes to a bigger and different reality. Community allowed me to begin grieving. I may be grieving for the rest of my life. But I feel like, for the first time, I can finally breathe. I am a newborn taking their first breath and screaming. I am a person who has been holding in the pain and grief. Each like a lace of the tightest corset, complete with real shortness of breath, dizziness and gendered expectations. Finding the right community has involved a group of femmes and thems gathering around me with the "good scissors" and cutting me out of that cruel lace.

Behind-the-Scenes

Ghostwriter
With the laces of false beliefs severed, I can finally breathe. Writing this essay broke me open. Writing this essay was my first foray into *actual* introspection. I was honestly quite surprised when I figured out that I had not been self-reflecting but instead had been self-policing all these years. Instead of feeling what I went through, I just told myself not to think about it. *It wasn't that bad, and other people have it worse, so suck it up.* Or, I would overanalyze my behavior,

connecting the dots with many "aha" moments, and filing my problems away as "dealt with." That is not healing. Healing is being seen and believed, and it has to start in me. This essay was the first time I told my story and was believed. It ruined me. To write it, I had to start feeling, truly embodying, the feelings of the last three decades. I started to dissociate more, losing track of time. Minutes, hours, days would go by in a blur. I kept waking up in the middle of a task I didn't remember starting. Waking up in the middle of conversations, unsure how I got there and what was being discussed. I was continuously waking up to reality, all of the realities extending from the past to the present. I was seeing and believing myself.

It is true that it is terrifying to be seen, so naked and beaten down. I can admit now that I am afraid of appearing weak, even if I was merely a child. Maybe that is why it has taken two years to complete and refine this. I have at least three different versions on what it was like to write about what kept me from writing, but no version is as authentic and connected as this. I spent most of my life pushing away the facts because I was taught that pain is weakness, and weakness is to be punished and humiliated.

Recently, I was asked to pick up the remnants of my childhood from his house. It looked almost exactly the same as I left it ten years ago with the exception of the addition of bags of birdseed tucked in between empty cardboard boxes. It looked like an abandoned museum of boxes. Some were half empty, some completely void, all with a thick layer of dust. The whiteboard in the kitchen remained untouched with the lyrics of "You Remind Me of the Babe," each line written by a different family member, an old family joke. The stacks of video games in front of the TV were a tower of filth, right where everyone left them. I launched from my body, watching it from afar. I watched as my meat suit sorted and trashed and packed. And now, I never have to see him again. Now, I can feel the pain and accept it as a part of me.

In the few memories worth keeping, I found photos of myself as a child. I saw myself, really looked at the pictures, and soaked it in. Years of parentification had distorted my view, which meant I have always seen myself as an adult. When I looked in the mirror, I would ask, "Is this really the body I am occupying?" and tap at the glass, waiting for the trick to end and my body to vanish or transform. It never added up to me. After writing this essay, which encapsulates what kept me from writing my whole life, I saw my humanity. And now, with a more complete picture, I could see that I was a child. This realization awakened the slumbering rage within.

Anger has been a hard-earned token. Anger transformed me into a capable person. It gave me these words. Words for my experience that has ignited a fire in my belly. A fire that consumes my flesh and soul in its sweet burning, sloughing off false beliefs layer by layer. Do not mistake me for a phoenix. I am of fire, but something different. I am mycelium and ash and the fertile soil of new life after a forest fire. My new life, my first real life, is not born from the cycles of my old; I have finally joined and become a part of life itself. I am a fungus feeding on the decay of the body of abuse cycles and transforming them into new life. New work. New beliefs. New practices.

The imposter syndrome comes and goes. I have learned that this is normal, and something to embrace. It does not have to be the dark hole of self-hatred that it used to be. As I learn to be my own parent, I have come to find that I am the only one who can cultivate the feelings of self-esteem, safety, and security within me. This is freeing and also horrifying. I think it is also real healing. Now, when self-doubt creeps in, I can hold the image of myself as a child with the image of the person I am creating and talk to these parts of myself as a gentle parent would. I mention how bravery is when we are scared, but we do it anyway. This is especially true in a safe and compassionate environment.

It was so hard to be seen and believed for the first time, and community is what made it possible. Communities are the testing ground, a point of transduction where ideas and beliefs about who we are become praxis. It scared me to the point that I just stopped writing. I stopped writing and I tried to deal like I always did, downplaying everything and isolating myself. The more I participated in the old stories about myself like this, the greater the distance became between having authentic relationships of any kind. I pushed everyone away. I had to change my entire life and way of being. I broke up with my partner, was victimized by someone calling me their friend who turned abusive and I left them behind, but I still couldn't connect to anyone in any meaningful way. Hurt people, hurt people, so they say, and I was bleeding all over everyone and everything I touched. I was perpetuating the very cycles from which I was trying to break free by overextending myself and people-pleasing. I was pandering to the imposter syndrome, feeding it and keeping it like a pet. Now that I am connecting with my authentic self, I can start to reconnect in real ways instead of through trauma bonds and dopamine. I am healing the parts that say, "This isn't good enough. I'm not good enough. Nobody cares." Shining a light on, listening to, and feeling why these messages are so deeply engrained has allowed me to let a lot of it go. Now, I just have to keep showing up.

The Vasectomy

By Tina Strawn

Sex.

Pregnancies.

Love.

Marriage.

Postpartum depression and psychosis.

Divorce.

Death.

An empty nest.

Bitterness. Anger. Resentment. Blame.

And a memory of a gesture of love.

This is my ex-wife grief.

———

Pregnant.

One time. With a condom.

What. The. Actual. Fuck.

That was me and my mom's reaction upon hearing the doctor at the clinic we went to in order to get medication prescribed for the chicken pox that I had somehow contracted at age 18.

Well, not those words exactly, because neither of us said

'fuck' at the time (though I now say it plenty enough for both of our lifetimes).

It made no sense.

We almost didn't believe this doctor.

"I can't give you any medication for your chicken pox because you are pregnant," the doctor said.

But how is that possible? my mom must have thought; this was her oldest daughter who she didn't even know was having sex.

The shock of this news likely hit her especially hard, because my younger, 16-year-old sister had just had a baby only a few short months earlier.

The confusion was there for me because…

Wait…

WE ONLY HAD SEX ONE TIME AND WE HAD USED A CONDOM.

So how could I be pregnant???

I delivered the news to him on Christmas Eve.

He was 21 years old, I was 18, and we had only dated for a few months.

He was planning on returning to school for his junior year of college after he worked to save up enough money to pay for it.

But now, he decided to join the U.S. Army to help cover the expenses of our unexpected-condom-miracle-baby that was on the way whether it made sense to us or not.

From the moment he enlisted, he set up an automatic payment to come directly to me of $250 every month.

He didn't demand proof of paternity.

I didn't have to take him to court to put him on child support.

We didn't even really know each other very well, having met September 4, 1995 and pregnant by the end of that same year.

But he started showing the kind of man he was with these very first gestures.

Integrity.

Responsibility.

Love.

So as I went through my first pregnancy, he went through basic training at Fort Jackson, South Carolina, and AIT at Fort Lee, Virginia.

Our daughter (who he, at one point, wanted to name Khadijah) was just a few weeks old when he held her for the first time, right before he shipped out to South Korea for his year-long tour of duty.

We were so young, and I had no idea what to expect from him, or from us.

Little did I know at the time, but this would be the beginning of our "beyond this lifetime" love story.

A love story through 11 years of marriage, three children.

A love story that has continued past our divorce.

A love story that has grown stronger even after his death.

———

26 years ago today, I went into labor because today was the day when you were ready to arrive and show up in the world, in all of your glory and majesty.

Though we didn't plan it that way, your father and I were both very happy and excited when we found out that we were pregnant with you. Your sister was almost 2 years old, and your father was a soldier in the US Army, stationed at Fort Riley, Kansas. I drove back and forth often from Dallas to spend the weekend with him in the barracks (which was very against the rules by the way). We were young and in love and getting pregnant with you was confirmation for us that we were ready to start a family and our lives together. It was time. We got married a few months later.

And a few months after that, I went into labor. Your father was nervous when I started having contractions, but he was so wonderful and so prepared. Yours was the easiest and fastest of my three labors. Your birth was pretty calm and peaceful as far as those things go, or maybe I'm just choosing to remember it that way. My mom was there, and so was her best friend (and the mother of 8 children) to help me with my labor.

I remember everyone coming to the hospital to see you…[both sets of your grandparents] and several of our friends. I remember your sister holding you delicately with Grandma's help. And I remember your father taking a picture with a cigar in his mouth that a friend brought him, but I don't think he smoked it lol. We were all overjoyed at your arrival.

The Vasectomy

A sad memory that I have is that 25 years ago today, I was hospitalized for postpartum depression and psychosis. At the time, I was pregnant with your brother, and your sister was only 3 years old, and we were poor, and my 22 year old body and mind was just overwhelmed and very tired, and so I missed your first birthday. Your dad bought you a little chocolate cake and he and your sister and a few friends were there to sing you happy birthday. He told me about it later and showed me pictures.

Thru the years, for some reason you always got the best birthdays. There were birthdays with tea parties and a petting zoo at our house, birthdays with Panda Bears and Build A Bears. And I'll never forget the house party we threw for your [S]weet 16. Our house was full of teenagers and that was kinda stressful lol, but it was also a lot of fun.

I don't remember all of your birthdays though, because we are only humans and we just aren't meant to remember everything, as much as we may want to. We are meant to keep making new memories and never stop making magical moments. We are meant to store what we can in our hearts and tell the stories to each other of what we remember throughout the years.

Everything has changed and life is very different now. You've been all grown up for a while now. All I am, all I have ever been, is a mother with a heart full of good intentions, hopes and dreams for the lives of you and your brother and sister, and also regrets. And yet still, I'm so thankful for all the years in between then and now.

I continue to cherish every single day that we get/got together, all that I remember and even what I don't. I believe it is all still there. All the long days and the short years remain stored somewhere deep in my heart, even the parts I forget. Such is the life of a human mother.

I have never been a perfect person. I am not a perfect woman, or a perfect mother or a perfect friend.

I am sorry for the many times I fell short of what you needed and wanted me to be.

All I can do is be here today or whenever you are ready. One thing I know for sure is that my favorite thing about my life is having the three of you in it. You and your brother and sister are the best things that have ever happened to me, the most miraculous and magical things your father and I have ever done. I am so proud of all of you every single day.
I miss you with my whole being, every part of me misses every part of you and your brother (and your dad). Your sister misses you too.

Happy birthday my beautiful, sweet nuunuu. I hope all of your birthday wishes come true.

I will keep loving you for the entirety of your life, and mine, and beyond.

January 13, 2025

———

By the time Chaz and I got married in 1998, we were pregnant with our second child, another daughter.

And just one month after I stopped breastfeeding her at nine months, I was pregnant with our third child, our son. When January 2000 rolled around, I was suffering from what they diagnosed as postpartum psychosis and depression, and I was admitted in-patient to a psych ward at a hospital in Fort Worth, Texas, where I would be on our second daughter's first birthday.

Pregnant with our son,

Being evaluated by doctors, nurses and therapists,

Prescribed Zoloft and Prozac,

And multiple private and group therapy sessions every day. After attempting to check myself out AMA (against medical advice), a court order was obtained to keep me there, as my medical team didn't think it was safe for me to be released.

I ultimately spent a few weeks there.

My very young, 22-year-old body and mind were just tired of being pregnant and poor.

Six months later, I gave birth to our son.

But despite the fact that I asked for my tubes to be tied, my doctor told me "no" and wouldn't perform the tubal ligation that I requested.

He said that I was too young to get my tubes tied because I "may want more children in the future."

I was 23 years old with three children.

But this doctor in Texas made the decision about my body and denied my choice of whether to have more children or not.

And that is when, in an unexpected turn of events,

My 25-year-old husband announced that he was going to go and get a vasectomy.

This was not a conversation that we had.

I had not asked this of him.

A vasectomy hadn't even crossed my mind. (I might not have even known what it was at the time.)

It was simply a decision that he came to and made on his own.

Saying that since I had carried and given birth to our three children,

He felt that it was now his responsibility to keep us from getting pregnant again.

So he would go and get a vasectomy since I couldn't get my tubes tied and so I wouldn't have to be on birth control and so we wouldn't have to use condoms for the rest of our lives.

And with that, it was done.

He went and got a vasectomy.

Simple and with no fanfare.

It wouldn't be until years later that I would fully appreciate this act of love.

It makes me wonder, for all the feminist men who love women and who care about reproductive justice, where is the vasectomy movement?

——

You say that sometimes you just need a mother, a parent. This is the first chance you've given me since October 2023. I'm here. Tell me what you need from me today.

I'm not traveling the world. These days I'm mostly at home just taking it day by day and trying to survive like everyone else.

I have found the peace I was looking for. And the healing. And the lessons. All still in progress. What have you found?

Your father and I were awful to each other after we divorced. I regret that and I'm so sorry that we didn't make dealing with our issues a priority and that we didn't see how much it hurt you all. Over the past several years, I have spent a lot of intentional time with him. He visits me often in so many ways...in dreams, as moths, on psilocybin and ayahuasca and other plant medicine journeys. We never hated each other. We loved each other very much but we also hurt each other. We were young lovers who became young parents and we got so caught up in our anger and grief and pain and confusion about how to live, how to take care of our family and survive, how to make sense of it all. We didn't give our best, not to each other, not to you and your brother and sister, not to ourselves. But we tried. Though we failed.

And then he died. And I lived. And I reconcile that every day. He is with me more now than he has ever been. He speaks to me even though you don't. But I believe one day that will change. I will be here when you are ready for that change.

Feb 11, 2025 - 10:27am

———

Sometimes it's hard being the one still here—the parent who lived long enough to hold the grief/anger/resentment/judgment meant for both of us.

The dead one becomes myth. The alive one becomes mirror.

One of us sainted, the other scorned.

Life and love.

Divorce and death.

Ex-wife grief and the irreconcilable nature of motherhood.

Behind-the-Scenes

I sat down for the first time to write my first draft for my submission at 7pm on May 24.

The due date of the submission was May 24.

I just noticed that I prefer the term 'due date' instead of 'deadline' because due date is kinder and I know Kim, our book coach and editor of this anthology, wants me to be kind to myself. I'm actually listening to the prep session replay right now about this essay writing process, and she just said, "Don't be hard on yourself."

So let's go back to when I first heard the assignment.

Write the thing you are most terrified to write. The thing you've been avoiding.

And my topics shifted from parenting when your kids are grown to ex-wife grief.

Until a lover went in to get a vasectomy.

And that made me remember when my ex-husband went and got a vasectomy.

And I immediately felt it was time to tell this story. This story of wisdom, care, sacrifice, strength, and love. I wanted to make the act of getting a vasectomy a beautiful and honorable thing. Because it was and still is.

So I began to write about all of that.

And I knew it in that moment: these were the things I was most terrified, and also most delighted, to write about. And that's when I realized that I was carrying so much grief about this season of parenting. I have an empty nest/heart, the father of my three children is dead, and two of my kids refuse to talk to me. (Meanwhile, my oldest daughter and I are best friends.)

I am sad that Chaz is gone, but I am also mad at him for leaving me to deal with the kids by myself. I am mad that he is not here to share the tremendous pride in them with me that only comes from being partners in bringing them into this world. I recognize this shitty feeling; it's a weird and random, yet true, shade of grief today.

And yes, I'm complaining right now about my deceased ex-husband and how he has it so easy because he's off somewhere in another dimension working on the next phase of his soul curriculum while I'm still here, all by myself, with these three little blessings that we brought into this realm together. Sometimes I do feel that way. I understand that talking shit about parenting is not a properly glamourizing position to take. But this is the reality of parenting no one talks about.

So here I am. 7:14 p.m. on deadline day.

Truth is, I almost gave up. I almost quit before I even started. I almost decided I just wasn't going to be able to write this thing. I had procrastinated masterfully ever since I agreed to participate. The concept was baking as I rolled the ideas in my head, but my body refused "butt to chair," and "words to Google Doc." But then I remembered the initial deadline—due date—I'd been given of May 24. For months I've sat on this and done nothing. *Can you not make this one deadline?* I wondered. *Can you at least do that for yourself and for your friend who is doing such a damn good job helping us become the writers we've all wanted to be?*

The process has gone from resentment to grief, back to love. And that is a great place to start and end. Because before it was divorce, it was marriage. And before my kids hated me, it was around me that they revolved. And there is a thread that runs through all of it. So I am choosing to write about the hard and scary parts of that thread.

I can do this one thing. So imperfect and rushed as it was, I turned in "The Vasectomy."

The Stories We Fear, the Words We Find

By Maria Wade

I USED TO BELIEVE THAT WRITING WAS ABOUT SKILL—TECHNI-cal mastery, grammar, structure. But the more I wrote, the more I realized that writing is about something else entirely: personal evolution. The words we put on the page are only as expansive as we are. Our limitations in writing are not about language proficiency or technique; they are about the boundaries of our own courage, self-perception, and willingness to be seen.

For years, my writing was shaped by a series of barriers, each more intricate than the last. The first was the simplest: language. English is not my native tongue, and the very idea of writing in it felt like walking a tightrope without a net. Every sentence, every word, was a battle with doubt. But I overcame it, as one does with any technical skill—with practice, guidance, and stubborn persistence. I told myself, "I may not write like a native speaker, but I can communicate my ideas well enough." And for a while, that sufficed.

Then came the next challenge: audience. Who was I writing for? Did anyone care? The silent, creeping fear that no one would read my words—or worse, that they would read them and dismiss them—almost silenced me.

But then I thought, "What if just one person cares? What if one person finds something useful or meaningful in my writing?" That was enough to keep going.

But writing is never just about skill or audience. It is about permission. What we allow ourselves to say. What we believe we are entitled to put into words. And this is where my real evolution began.

Writing the Unwritable

There were stories I had long avoided, topics I danced around as if they were fire. One of them was my hearing impairment. For years, I thought writing about it would expose me, make me vulnerable in ways I wasn't prepared for. It felt like revealing a weakness, like inviting pity. I wasn't seeking validation or sympathy. But as I grew in my writing, I realized that any limitation—physical, emotional, social—is only as limiting as our response to it. My hearing impairment was not a flaw; it was a part of my experience. It shaped me, yes, but it did not define me.

When I finally decided to write about my hearing impairment, I sat with the draft for weeks. It was ready, polished even. But still, it remained unpublished. I kept asking myself: *What am I really afraid of?* The answer wasn't exposure—it was permanence. Once those words were out in the world, I couldn't take them back. The vulnerability would be fixed in place. But I also realized that by not publishing it, I was letting fear decide what parts of my story were shareable. Writing about it was, ultimately, about owning my narrative, about showing that resilience is not about denial but about choice. The essay is written, ready. With this new perspective, it now sits in my drafts not because I lack courage, but because I chose to focus first on my book. And that choice, too, is an act of ownership—deciding not just what to write, but when to release it into the world.

But personal vulnerability, I discovered, was only one kind of challenge. Writing about my hearing impairment affected only how people saw me. Then I began experiencing the shifts that come with transitioning to the next stage of life as a woman—the physical changes, the impact on my work, the adjustment required. As I searched for guidance, I found mostly silence in leadership circles. When the topic of menopause *was* discussed, it was framed as something that required accommodation, special treatment. I disagreed. I wanted to write about menopause in professional settings differently. But the stakes were higher than writing about my own hearing impairment. This could affect how people saw *all* women leaders. Would my words reinforce biases rather than dismantle them? Would they make it harder for women leaders rather than easier?

The silence around menopause in leadership spaces isn't accidental—it's strategic. Women fear that acknowledging biological changes will confirm stereotypes about female unreliability. I had to decide: Would I contribute to that silence, or would I show another way? The answer lay in perspective. Instead of framing menopause as a challenge that required external validation or support, I wrote about it as an opportunity for self-leadership—a transition we navigate through our own agency rather than something done to us. The writing was no longer about seeking understanding from others. Instead, it was about empowering those experiencing it. The piece is written, ready. But I haven't released it yet. Not from fear, but from intention. Some words need the right context, the right moment, to land as intended. And with that shift in focus, the fear dissolved.

The Story I Refuse to Tell

There is one story I have not written. My immigration story. Not because it is too painful, or too private, but because it no longer defines me. I am not my past, no matter how dramatic, how compelling it may be. My story is not about what I left behind but about what I am building now. Writing about my immigration feels like placing my past at the center of my narrative, overshadowing everything I have created since. That, I will not do.

This decision is not made out of fear, but as a clear, intentional choice. Not everything needs to be written, at least not in this moment. And recognizing that, too, is a kind of evolution.

Writing for the Algorithm vs. Writing for Meaning

For years, I tried to do what everyone said I should: post regularly, feed the algorithm, stay visible. I wrote on schedule, crafted posts designed for engagement, followed the formulas. And the response was... muted. Polite likes, perhaps, but no real connection.

Then I stopped. I decided I would only write when I had something meaningful to say—not to the algorithm, but to myself. When an idea seized me, when I couldn't *not* write about something. The cadence became irregular, unpredictable. And something unexpected happened. People started responding differently. Not just with likes, but with messages. They'd reference something I'd written weeks or months ago in our conversations. They'd say, "That thing you wrote about your experience of becoming an empty nester—I've been thinking about it." My words weren't disappearing into the feed; they were landing, sticking, resonating.

I learned that consistency without authenticity is just noise. But authenticity—even irregular, even infrequent—creates connection. The algorithm wants content. People want truth.

Behind-the-Scenes

Every writer, at some point, faces similar questions: Who am I to write this? Will anyone care? Is this even worth putting into words? I am no exception. For a long time, I struggled with the idea that I was not a "real" writer. I am a coach, a thinker, a speaker. This is precisely why my avoided topic is about grappling with my writer identity. Writing was something I did, not something I was. I would sit in writing circles, surrounded by "real" writers, and feel like an imposter.

Real writers, I thought, wrote daily. They had discipline, routines, word counts. They fed the algorithm, built audiences, maintained momentum. When I couldn't do that—when I could only write when something required to be written—I saw it as a failure. But perhaps it wasn't. Perhaps the distinction between "being a writer" and "writing" is exactly this: writers write when they must, not when they should.

There is a strange transformation that happens when we admit we are writers. It is an identity shift, a way of seeing ourselves. I used to say, "I am not a writer." Then I shifted to, "I write." Now, with a published book and words that people carry with them long after reading, I understand: I became a writer, and not through consistency, but through honesty.

But even with this shift, the fears persist. The doubts linger. The voice in the back of my mind whispers, "What if this is the essay that finally exposes you as a fraud?" The irony is that writing is, by nature, *exposure*. It is standing on a stage, microphone in hand, and saying, "This is what I think. This is what I believe." And hoping, praying, that someone in the audience nods in understanding.

Yet, there is freedom in that, too. Writing, for me, is not about perfection. It is about exploration. About stretching the limits of my own thinking, challenging myself to articulate ideas that feel just out of reach. It is not about proving that I belong, but about discovering who I am. And if one person reads this and sees themselves in my words, then it was worth it. But here's what I've learned: when we write from genuine need rather than perceived obligation, when we prioritize meaning over metrics, something shifts. Our words don't just reach people—they stay with them. They become part of conversations, touchstones for thinking differently.

So, I write. Not daily, not on schedule, not to feed an algorithm. I write when I have something that demands to be said, when the cost of silence exceeds the cost of exposure. I write to discover what I think, to push against my own boundaries, to claim the parts of my story I'm ready to own. And in those moments of authentic expression, I'm not performing writership. I'm simply a writer, doing what writers do.

Limitations be damned.

Permission to Be

By Becka Eppley

"I NEED TO TELL YOU SOMETHING."

Sitting in my "cloffice" (closet office) situated just inside our guest bedroom door, I heard him coming up the stairs and walking through the next room. My heart was pounding. I knew once I told him, there was no going back. I called out his name. "I need to tell you something." I turned my chair around, stood up, and walked towards him. I took a deep breath and said, "I think I am bisexual… I mean, I know I am. It doesn't change anything though," I said, an attempt at reassuring us both. "I still love you. I just wanted you to know."

After a very brief pause, he responded positively. He was good with me identifying as bisexual, he said. He let me know that, in fact, he believed a lot of people are probably bisexual, however, they may not come out because our culture doesn't give us the freedom to just be who we are. I was relieved at his response, and yet I had a creeping feeling in the pit of my stomach that I was not revealing to him—or admitting to myself—my whole truth.

In fifth grade, I liked boys because I thought that's what girls were supposed to do. Liking boys felt like another obligation to my young mind. There was nothing natural about it to me. However, it seemed not only to be a mandated social cue among my group of friends but also the narrative throughout my family home. My mind would twist and contort my inner dialogue, trying to come up with logical reasons for why I could/should have a crush on certain male-identifying people. Most of those narratives revolved around the idea that if I were to be a wife and mother, I would need a man to take care of me and our family financially. I did my best to be an obedient child, to be a rule follower, and to learn how a "Godly Wife" acts so that I would be desirable to a "Godly Man." Even at a young age, I was thinking about marriage, and the indoctrination of patriarchal narratives was already running swiftly through the synapses in my brain. So when my friends began getting crushes on boys, I followed suit.

I grew up in a very insulated religious bubble. Despite spending a good portion of my formative years on the coast of central California, my exposure to anyone not identifying as cisgender and heterosexual was practically non-existent. When you combine my lack of exposure to the LGBTQIA2S+ community, religious conditioning, and being a child who experienced high levels of anxiety, the layers of confusion built upon my understanding of who I was (and am) might as well have equated to a towering volcano.

A sense of unease was constantly roiling beneath the surface, just out of reach of my conscious awareness. That creeping feeling in the pit of my stomach I mentioned? That was pretty normal. And yet, more than two years after I disclosed my "truth" to my then-husband, that feeling remained buried. Not only did it stay buried, but repeated circumstantial struggles seemed to pile more and more on top of it, as I operated daily in a state of mental and emotional survival mode.

On the afternoon of January 14, 2023, I spent time with a close friend at a local tea apothecary. The vibe in this particular tea bar is hard to find elsewhere: they intentionally do not offer WIFI and encourage everyone to unplug and be present. I spent the afternoon sharing how trapped I felt in my marriage. I had no idea how to move forward. At the end of our three-hour conversation, my friend looked at me and asked, "Do you believe that the universe conspires in your favor?" I paused and thought.

"I truly do not know," I finally replied. We then got up, returned our uniquely designed teapots to the serving station and walked outside towards my friend's car. There was a small labyrinth amongst the pine trees situated beside the car, and we stopped to take it in. As we drove away, I felt encouraged and held by my friend, though at the same time my hope was waning. The hope that things in my marriage could actually improve, the hope that the unearthing of who I have always been would require little more than a private conversation with tears falling into a cup of tea.

The air outside my home felt thick that night, and the

energy was heavy. As I entered through the front door, I greeted my husband and asked if he was okay. My husband's parents had 'spontaneously' agreed to take the kids for the weekend and so he and I were the only ones in the house.

He responded with his usual, "Work is stressful right now."

A few hours later he would tell me he was done with our marriage.

Looking back, that moment felt like an eruption, magma everywhere. It was like the ash from Mount Saint Helens when she erupted in 1980, covering my childhood home in Montana and everything as far as the eye could see. That, as they say, was that. With six words—"I am done with our marriage"—we went from sharing a bed and kissing goodnight, to separate rooms and to never touch again, all within a span of seconds. That first night, in a state of shock, I cried myself to sleep.

Over the next eight months, I would experience one curveball after another, so much so that my close friends continually expressed how baffled they were at the sheer volume of shit coming my way. I spent many days feeling numb, so when the next shitty thing happened, I had no emotions left to even let the circumstantial crisis phase me. I survived those months with the support of my chosen family, my younger brother, and my therapist.

I spent seven of those eight months continuing to cohabitate with my now ex-husband. The daily tension was palpable. When he asked me for a divorce, he already had plans in place for how he would like to move forward. One of those plans involved me moving out.

The transition to two separate households was not easy. Our marriage ended in the very same house where we'd brought my daughter home from the hospital. My son was very young when we'd moved in, and it was the only home he had ever known. I had poured blood, sweat, and tears into the interior of the house. I painted almost every room from a cold gray to a warm sand color. I removed mirror plating from an entire wall, patched it, and added fresh paint. The list of changes went on, but none of that seemed to matter anymore. It was his late grandfather's former house, and I didn't have a say.

With the help of chosen family, friends, and co-workers, I eventually found a new place to live, one that was just right for the kids and me. It was a cute yellow house in a quiet neighborhood. It had a sunroom that my plants could bask in during the colder months and a screened-in porch. Unbeknownst to me at the time, that porch would soon become a place of healing and late night snuggles with the moon.

I worked diligently to create that "homey" feeling my children had grown up with. A feeling of welcome and invitation to come and stay a while. Why use overhead lighting when a room full of lamps with a soft yellow glow makes me feel cozy no matter the season? "Homey" for me is a space where I am not afraid to spill a drip of coffee, and there are comfortable places to lounge at almost every turn. In the last several years, I have come to realize how important it is to me that wherever I reside, it will be a safe space, a space of reprieve. When friends and family are in my home, I desire for them to feel peaceful, like they are receiving a warm hug for the soul. My home is my sanctuary.

So, for the first few months, I spent most of my non-working hours getting our new home ready. However, no matter how much effort I put in, this house was still not the home that my children had grown up in; adjustment takes time. Creating sanctuary is not only an aesthetic but the releasing of what was and the welcoming of possibility. It is giving oneself *permission to be.*

Permission to be. With this new freedom, I now had the time and was able to give myself permission to process more of what it meant for me to identify as bisexual. In many ways, it felt like I was sifting through a lifetime of proverbial dirt that had been piled upon the deep knowing of who I truly am. I now sat with a new question. *Am I really bisexual, or am I a lesbian?*

The more I thought about it and the more I processed my thoughts with my therapist and friends, I knew the answer. Of course, I had doubts on a daily basis after coming to this life-changing conclusion at the age of 46. I had never dated a woman, let alone kissed a woman. How could I know that my feelings were not just a response to a cisgender, heterosexual marriage that had come to end? I thought back again to fifth grade. I thought about how, even at such a young age, I believed boys were a means to an end, that they were obligatory.

Acknowledging to myself that I was a lesbian was liberating. For the first time in over 40 years, it felt good to be in my own skin. My first experience with love and heartbreak came quickly, and with it came further affirmation that I was indeed on the right path. I experienced a jolt of confidence even in the midst of it all. For the first time in my life, I realized that heartbreak wasn't a result of being undesirable but rather a lack of compatibility.

My self-assurance did not magically appear once I finally admitted to myself that I was, and had always been, a lesbian. In fact, I am not sure I would have uncovered my sexual orientation in such a freeing way if I had not started to deconstruct my evangelical faith upbringing years earlier on the cusp of my 30th birthday. That ongoing journey started the process of clearing internal space that had previously been consumed with religious dogma, anxiety, and guilt.

During my faith deconstruction I listened, watched, and observed many people question their knowing of who they are. I came to a realization that there are many similarities between the cultures of evangelicalism and capitalism. Both require you to follow predetermined steps in order for you to reach an end goal that supports the longevity of their existence within a given society. Both are willing to sacrifice people and resources for the sake of the "greater good." Both are founded on principles of heteronormativity. In fact, these principles of heteronormativity are what my aging parents cling to daily.

As a result, my own self-confidence has been crucial. Six months after coming out publicly, I came out to my mom. I shared with her that I have more peace now as a lesbian than I ever had before and that I am so thankful for my divorce. I was met with the following response: "It grieves us and God. I have no doubt you are enjoying life right now because sin does have its season of enjoyment, until it doesn't. We will always love you and so will God."

I am grateful that, despite her lack of acceptance, my mom still loves me. I am also grateful that I am hearing her words now, in my 40s, because I wonder if my teenage self would have spiraled deeper into an already-present suicidal ideation. If her words had come at a time when I didn't have the tools I have now (including a therapist and anxiety medication), and was simply told to "pray about it," the outcome might have been different.

I spent 45 years trying to figure out how to feel good in my own skin. Then, less than a year after my ex-husband declared he was done with our marriage, all the narratives I had sought refuge in for decades were literally torn apart. The process of unearthing who I had always been felt both abrupt and overwhelming in the most beautiful and daunting ways. My friend and I now joke that when they asked me that afternoon over tea if I believed that the Universe conspires in my favor, the Universe said, "It's time to get the fuck out Becka!"

I believe what I experienced in the first four decades of my life was *Compulsory Heterosexuality* or *Comphet* for short. It is "the theory that heterosexuality is assumed and enforced upon people by a patriarchal and heteronormative society." Much like my ongoing journeys of faith deconstruction and self-assurance, I also began learning to recognize my internal narratives around heteronormativity and homophobia. Often, the unlearning was—and still is—overwhelming. For me, however, each of these journeys is essential; they are paths that lead to one another. At times, the paths intertwine, overlap, and sometimes they flow side by side. I used to feel great fear when I couldn't understand or predict where or when a path would end. Now, more often than not, I experience great freedom because there is no final destination. I am learning to find joy in infinite growth and exploration.

Part of my growth on these journeys of self-exploration has been learning to acknowledge that I have a power and strength that are uniquely my own. However, I am realizing that discovering something new about oneself is rarely cut and dry. While I feel good in my skin and have given myself *permission to be* who I am, I sometimes find myself scared of my own power.

My fear tends to show up after I outwardly express newfound confidence, leaving me with a feeling of "too muchness." When I began dating AFAB (assigned female at birth) people, I would get back in my car after an outing—a date, or an event—and find myself feeling unsettled. The narratives of patriarchy always seemed to remind me that my power wasn't real power but rather pridefulness, cockiness, or me taking up too much space. My therapist would later remind me that what I was experiencing was actually confidence, something I'm still learning to accept about myself.

The power I feel inside is not something new; I have experienced it since I was a young child, this surge of knowing that there is something greater within me. However, I learned to be afraid of it, to believe that it made me a threat to my religious beliefs, and that the power was not actually me but the Holy Spirit. When I showed up with confidence as a child, I interpreted my parents' response to me as though they did not know what to do with me. I wanted my parents to make me feel safe, so I made myself feel small. The power I felt internally was constantly clashing with the indoctrination I was trying to live out. I can now see this was all a catalyst for a good portion of the anxiety I experienced as a child and still do to this day. However, living into my authenticity—which includes identifying as a lesbian—has encouraged me to no longer make myself small and to welcome the power that has always lived within me.

I want to live from the core belief of welcoming my power on a daily basis. I desire to feel joy when I step into it and not immediately run through a list of scenarios about what it might cost me in that moment. I have to remind myself every day that journeys are not finite. That birth is a necessary transition from a space of 'known' variables to one of unlimited possibilities. That giving myself *permission to be* is one of the greatest forms of self-love I can experience.

Behind-the-Scenes

Often our desires to share our journeys and experiences are halted quickly by external narratives that tell us we do not know enough, we have not lived enough, we have not... fill-in-the-blank. Western culture curates the belief that if we are not experts in a field then we have nothing to bring to the proverbial table, or what we do have to bring lacks any sort of value. My heart and mind know that these perspectives are not true, yet they often linger around the edges of my knowing as I write. While writing this essay, these perspectives not only appeared but, many times, tried to intercede.

For me, perfectionism goes hand and hand with expertise. They are a bitter couple hiding in the corner of my brain, whispering snarky comments to each other just loud enough for me to hear. Their comments created doubt. I wrote half of my essay and then completely scrapped it once new life experiences happened, bringing about new perspectives.

There is a narrative in my head that whatever I write has to be the "truest version," the most "correct version." Growing up in a religious household, we were taught to believe that whatever someone wrote down was their *whole truth and nothing but the truth*. That those words would always be where they lived and spoke from. It was not until I was an adult—and I don't mean when I turned 18 or when my brain was fully developed in my twenties; I mean my late thirties—that I could grasp the idea that people wrote from a perspective of where they were at a particular point in their journey. That the ideas, hopes, dreams, and perspectives of an author more than likely had evolved since they wrote the piece I was reading.

I now firmly believe that the journeys of unearthing, such as faith deconstruction and self-assurance, are never finite. I don't believe that any of us can ever reach a definitive conclusion on any state of personal evolution, just as we cannot lay claim to another human being, the land we live on, or the patterns of the stars.

Writing about being a late in life lesbian brought up a lot of insecurity for me. When I started writing this essay, I had only been out publicly as a lesbian for less than six months. I was worried about what the LGBTQIA2S+ community would think of me. I had spent 46 years as a racialized white, cisgender, heterosexual female with all the privileges that those identities bring with them, especially living in the United States. My imposter syndrome was strong while writing, and the bitter couple in the corner of my brain was cheering it on. I had to make daily choices to trust myself, to remember who I am and why I am sharing this part of myself. Some days I did not succeed at making these choices; some days I wanted to keep my writing to myself.

One of my core personal beliefs is that all human beings are connected whether or not we can (or choose to) see that connection. One of my offerings towards creating and continuing connectivity is to share my journey through writing. I am not sharing because my journey is "the best" or because I believe my writing will resonate with every person who picks it up. I am sharing because if one other human being feels seen, encouraged, or affirmed in who they are, that is enough. Would I love it if my writing encouraged thousands of people? Absolutely! However, grandeur is not my goal or desired arrival point. I don't believe there is anything wrong with experiencing "success," however it is often birthed in the ideals of capitalism and the cost often comes at the expense of human connectivity, the state in which I believe we thrive most.

When we are striving for this connectivity, I believe it is also important to acknowledge that each person's view of the world is seen through a lens that is unique solely to them. We can share similar values and have experiences that seem to parallel one another; however, how we ingest and take in the world is done so through a distinctive lens that only comes from our individual lived experiences. I would like to offer an expanded viewpoint of the word "lens" from that pertaining only to the human eye, to more of an embodied definition. When I think of my own personal lens, I think of it as a filter by which sights, sounds, touch, and feelings come through and are experienced in my being.

In my essay, I share parts of my story of coming out as a late in life lesbian. My experiences, however, are not penned to be universal truths; they came to me through my own personal evolution. Even as I write these words, I know that tomorrow, and for many days to come, I will need to continue to remind myself that my experiences hold value, that they are part of what brought me to you, dear reader, and that they are intertwined with your experiences to draw us together as a human collective.

How Grief Stole My Religion

By Amanda Conley Hines

WHETHER YOUR LOSS INVOLVES A RELATIONSHIP, A SEASON OF peace, your childhood, a body free from pain, or the transition of a loved one, grief is a kaleidoscope of varying colors and brilliance.

My name is Amanda, and I grew up in a Baptist church in Louisiana. I say "grew up" because my dad was a devoted deacon who made sure we were present for Sunday service, prayer meetings, and sometimes business meetings. While I may not have understood religious nuances in my youth, in Sunday School I learned about God's power, affirmation, and love. He created flowers, trees, stars, and animals and took the time to declare them *good*. To me, God was Abba—a powerful but caring *Father*. Imagine the joy and affirmation I felt at being a part of God's creations. I adored Him with all my heart. Although most considered the church to be God's house, I preferred connecting with Him in a field near my home. Laying in the prickly grass, I imagined Father's face just beyond the cerulean sky as I revealed my heart with open trust.

I cherished those sacred times in that field for many years. Until I grew older. Until I overheard conversations in religious circles about the more punishing and wrathful side of my loving Creator. A Supreme Being who held a set of *worthy* and *unworthy* scales embossed with my name. Soon, my trust became fear. Billboards haunted me with messages like, "If Jesus were to come back right now, would you go to heaven or hell?" I caught glimpses of Judgment Day booklets inundated with graphic images of souls tormented by fire. This evolution, though jarring, felt fitting. Scripture says when you are a child, you think like a child, but there comes a time to put away childish ways. Apparently, my earlier understanding of God was based on naïve ideologies.

This transition in awareness was my first experience with grief. Religion represented two central realities: *a penal system* focused heavily on what not to do to remain in God's good graces and *a transactional system* whereby you do good so God will hear and answer your prayers. As this distinction became clear, I quickly lost the concept of merely basking in my Creator's love; instead, I needed to earn His acceptance through fear and trembling. Open trust became a distant pinpoint on the horizon. My visits to our field became less frequent. The sky felt oppressive now, like a magnifying glass, and the once-bright, pulsating tendrils of a loving relationship transformed into the iron-clad chains of "religion."

———

Certain milestones defined 2017 for me. The first was my fortieth birthday in March. In April that year, I was in my kitchen, more than a thousand miles from my small hometown village in Louisiana, when my mom called and uttered the words that altered everything: "Mandy, your daddy has cancer." Mom and Dad reassured me. "Everything will be fine, Mandy. We have to have faith." I understood what they meant; faith is the substance of things hoped for when the evidence remains hidden. I asked the appropriate questions about the next steps. However, once the call ended, the rational adult in me took a back seat. My knees buckled, and my ill-prepared inner child emerged as I cried out, "Please, God, don't take my daddy!"

I screamed towards heaven until my throat burned, and my hiccups felt more like gagging. Looking back, the initial crack in my foundation revealed itself when I wondered what Daddy had done to anger God. God's anger was the only rational explanation for this situation. But how could that be? Mack Conley was a faith-filled, hard-working, generous, loyal, kind, and patient man who dedicated his life to helping others. As with Job in the Bible, clearly this was a test of his faith. Our faith.

The Bible defines faith in Hebrews 11:1 as *confidence in what we hope for and assurance about what we do not see*. I needed to believe that God would heal my daddy.

So that's what I did, or at least I tried. I cried out to Heaven on his behalf daily. I declared the promises in the scriptures over my dad. I played gospel music on a loop and paid careful attention to my words, reminding myself that the Bible says death and life are in the power of the tongue.

I was a mess. As days turned into months, I found myself in a daze, shuffling one foot in front of the other and trying my best to plug the emotional holes that formed.

There's a verse in the Bible about how mustard seed-sized faith can move mountains, but fear and anxiety plucked at the seams of my mustard seed bag. Scripture states it is impossible to please God without faith, and I couldn't bear the thought of being the reason my daddy didn't get healed, so I borrowed faith from others, asking them to leverage their prayers to fill my gaps.

—

On September 6, two weeks after my last visit, Mama told me I needed to come home again. I flew back the following day, unprepared for what lay ahead. I felt like Alice, not in Wonderland, but dropped into a parallel universe where nothing mattered beyond the next second. All time markers disappeared in the days that followed; every minute became a montage of sounds, scents, and images. Daddy's labored breathing and the rattle of phlegm in his throat as he tried to clear it. The aroma of cold-pressed olives from the anointing oil lingered in the air, a testament to our fervent prayers for him. Daddy always smelled of sandalwood, not because of cologne but because of a lifetime spent among fragrant timber at the wood mill. Now, the stench of cancer marred that familiar scent. I felt an unfamiliar weight as I held Daddy's hand, reversing our roles. I stared at him for hours, memorizing every pore and rogue hair sprouting outside his always perfectly trimmed goatee. The urge to shave those offending hairs was strong, but the time for such trivialities had passed. The pumping motion of his heart pulsed through an abnormal gap between the fourth and fifth ribs. I never knew of that defect because the muscles of a healthy man hid the vulnerability. Lying next to him, I willed his heart to keep pumping. By the evening of September 8, Daddy was nonverbal, and I mourned the loss of his husky laughter and words of wisdom. The day before, he had held both my sister's hand and my hand, using his waning strength to pray for ours. I must have told him I loved him a hundred times just to hear him say, "I love you too, Mandy."

On September 9, I woke up next to my dad, having slept beside him for two nights. My sister swapped places with me at 7:50 a.m., and I went to sit outside on the porch with my mom, whose strength during all of this continues to amaze me. We sipped coffee for 1,800 seconds before my sister screamed.

Well-meaning people said: "He's in a better place," "Don't question God," and "God gives and takes away."

———

After the initial, shock-induced numbness came a five-year looping trek through the five stages of grief.

Denial: The neurons in my brain, committed to the 40-year relationship with my dad, refused to register the loss. They just kept firing regardless of the *'not found'* message, keeping me in a forever state of panic. This restless energy followed me into my dreams, where I experienced a cycle of trying to save Daddy from death's plans. Still, every time I saved him from one fate, the one that came after was always worse.

Anger: This wasn't supposed to happen! Daddy was supposed to get better. We prayed the prayers, cried the tears, recited the scriptures, and gave thanks in advance for his testimony of healing. Yet, despite it all, he was gone. I felt betrayed, abandoned, and furious—caught in a relentless game of Red Rover between anger and despair.

Bargaining: I became hyper-fixated on what went wrong. Why did God not accept my prayers? Was my anxiety seen as a lack of faith? Did I not pray the right words? What if I missed asking forgiveness for a sin? There must be something I could do over again.

Depression: Before losing my dad, I would have described grief as deep sadness. But that's like calling the ocean a puddle. Grief is more than sorrow; it's a poltergeist demanding space, consuming everything in its path—an intruder, leaving smudges and fingerprints on every cherished memory. I wandered aimlessly through a dense fog, colliding with reminders of what I had lost. My smiles were simple muscle memory, because grief breaks the hand that holds joy.

Acceptance: A friend once described her place in God's Kingdom as being in the room with Him, yet sitting in the corner—present but unseen without a voice or consideration. That sentiment resonated deeply with me.

In the Bible, a story about the death of Jesus' friend Lazarus highlights the contrasting grief of his sisters, Mary and Martha. Though devastated, Martha accepted her brother's loss, clinging to the hope of seeing him again in Heaven. Mary, however, was too shattered to think about the afterlife. Her anguish spilled into her words as she cried, "If you had been here, he wouldn't have died." I understood Mary. I, too, sat in the corner, feeling broken and overlooked, trying to convince myself that, while *God gives and takes away*, His plan was far greater than my pain.

———

Typically, people will offer condolences for a few weeks before their words fade into silence, and to cling to that grief means doubting God and His plan. Yes, I've heard it said. But how can you attach a healing timeline to the violent severing of a heart tether?

I've seen and felt wonders defying explanation, so I never considered becoming an atheist or agnostic, but I no longer prayed with any real expectation. Why should I? I had proof that God wasn't listening to me. The memory of me as that little girl in the field seemed like a work of fiction.

For years, I continued to put one foot in front of the other because I had to. My husband needed me, my babies needed me, and my mom and sister needed me, so I dutifully slipped into my roles while silently choking on my grief. I was Job—a man in the Bible who had everything stripped from him as a test of faith. Alone and isolated, I'd become orphaned by a God I'd loved and spent my entire life serving, maybe not perfectly, but serving nonetheless.

———

During one of my treks through the depression stage, questioning many things, I became friends with a woman named Jen Kinney, who was on a journey of deconstructing her faith. I had never encountered this concept before, but it would change *everything*. Yes, deconstruction has its extremes. Still, at its core, it involves reexamining your beliefs to uncover the truth while discarding manmade traditions, misinterpretations, and outright falsehoods. As a starting point, Jen suggested a teaching by Shane Willard entitled "How to Read the Bible Like a Hebrew." This teacher seemed to imply a more profound understanding to be gained beyond simply picking up the Bible and reading it.

Reading the biblical text through the perspective of its authors made sense, so I watched the video—and then several more. What was so compelling? Well, remember Job? The book of Job begins with a 'scene in heaven' where Satan meets with God. God speaks of His servant Job, but Satan scoffs, suggesting that Job is only 'faithful' because he has everything he wants. In response, God agrees to let Satan take everything away from Job to prove a point. Harsh, right? This account made God seem capricious with our lives, yet expecting our devotion.

I learned two important things about the Book of Job. First, the author is unknown. Second, and more importantly, it falls under wisdom literature or poetry. This means readers should interpret the Book of Job metaphorically, not literally. Exiled people grappling with why bad things happen wrote Job. While this distinction may seem minor to some, it changed my imagination of God's character.

As my deconstruction journey continued, I recalled something my pastor, Beau McCarthy, once said: "Everything in the Bible is a journey towards Jesus." The Bible points towards salvation. Shane Willard also mentioned that Jesus is the embodiment of God's character. This inspired me to look for representations of God in Jesus' actions, and I found those examples.

For instance, even though the law mandated the stoning of women caught in adultery, Jesus chose to show compassion. When I read about the Samaritan woman at the well or the parable of the Good Samaritan, I discovered how taboo and controversial Jesus' actions were during that time. It's akin to a white person socializing with a person of color during the Jim Crow era. The Samaritans were viewed as unclean because of their mixed heritage—half Jewish and half Gentile. Temple authorities forbade the Samaritans, foreigners, the sick, prostitutes, the "lame," and the blind—people on the fringes—from entering. Even the poor were relegated to only certain areas, yet Jesus reached out to all of them. Healed them. Loved them. Jesus was the harshest to those who thought they were better than others and those who used scriptures to exclude. Jesus taught us to have mercy over judgment.

Let's revisit the story of Mary and Martha. Another verse caught my attention: "Jesus wept." It's the shortest verse in the Bible, and I've read it countless times, but I overlooked its significance. Now, it was all I could see. Jesus didn't reprimand Mary for her words; instead, He grieved with her. How did I miss the significance of this verse? It encapsulates everything! This was the Abba I knew when I lay in that field—a loving Father who would mourn with two sisters even though He would bring their brother back to life.

Losing my dad shattered my heart, but even more devastating was the perceived rejection, condemnation, and abandonment from God. Studying the Bible through the lens of cultural context, genre, and history made me realize how limited my perspective was and how Westernized religion had constrained my understanding of God. Like someone gradually regaining feeling in a paralyzed limb, I experienced subtle, unfiltered spiritual awakenings and divine synchronicity.

———

This is not the end of my grief journey. How could it be when the love for my dad intertwines with the pain of the loss? However, I don't feel ashamed, faithless, or condemned because I continue to grieve, nor do I sit in a corner, unconsidered. Nor do I obey God out of fear of His wrath or hell anymore; instead, I serve Him by serving others because His abundant grace, love, and mercy make me want to emulate Him. I can reach toward Heaven again because I feel Father's love and connection. I am not alone in hopeless despair anymore.

Despite being a bruised and scarred version of that child lying in the field, I once again have hope. Because of this, I find comfort in knowing my dad isn't alone in the ether somewhere, nor does he cease to exist; he is with his loving Creator. When I say that grief stole my religion, I mean it broke the framework I was taught God worked within. But God is bigger than that.

Yes, grief has stolen my religion, but it also resurrected the little girl in me who can once again gaze into the sky with an open heart.

Behind-the-Scenes

I felt tangible fear and trepidation when saying yes to this project. I'm a fiction writer; being asked to write a non-fiction piece fueled the incessant rantings of imposter syndrome. My husband, bless his heart, wanting to be supportive says, "They thought you were worthy of asking, so believe them." Instead of just accepting his words, I push back with a reframe: "You love golf. Let's pretend someone asks you to play in a PGA tournament. How would you feel? Knowing everyone is watching and comparing you to better players." It was gratifying to see his face flush and his throat bob as he grasped the weight of my anxiety. But then I realized I had made it even more tangible for myself.

The other writers contributing to this project are masters of voice, consistently leading readers on compelling journeys. Some write professionally. I'm a 47-year-old woman with ADHD and a people-pleasing addiction I'm actively recovering from. Though I love writing, I carry a bulging filing cabinet of intrusive thoughts. I experience the typical "I'm not good enough" anxieties when sharing any of my writing. But there's more: What if I give away some of my secrets in my writing? What if someone says, "This character is clearly the author exorcising her demons"? What if people hate the character and, by extension, hate me? Is this in my voice, or am I mimicking someone else? Will others judge me if they meet me and point out everything wrong with my work or how they would've done it differently?

The invitation for this project was to share a part of myself that I've never shared before, something important to me that I've never put to paper. I immediately knew what story wanted to be told. So, like a coward, I wrote about something else. I wrote about the birth of my oldest daughter, Mia. My blood mixed with hers created bilirubin issues and, as a result, I came home from the hospital with a deflated belly and empty arms. Yes, this was a deeply personal moment in my life, one that I held deep grief over. When I finished, however, I realized I was already on the other side of that grief and guilt, so it felt like a phone-in effort to an enormous opportunity. I needed to go deeper.

Writing this piece was like trying to pour fifty gallons of content into a two-ounce container. When it comes to the "plotter" versus (flying-by-the-seat-of-your-pants) "pantser" dichotomy, I'm a classic methodological pantser*—I often write the bones, add meat, and then trim the fat on a different device. More often than not, I end up scrapping the trimmed portion in favor of the original

---

* Ellen Brock. (2020, January 31). *The Four Types of Novel Writers*. YouTube.

version. I need to see something on the page to work out the kinks and direction.

This time, though, even the "bone version" felt uncomfortable. Adding details felt like flaying myself. Going back and forth through the editing process was like trying to tape pieces of myself back together. It was hard to encapsulate seven years of emotional and spiritual discovery into 3,000 words. Each writing session left me feeling bloody and bruised. I went to the deepest, darkest places in the recesses of my mind, pouring out every traumatic memory and using all five senses to paint a high-definition portrait of my grief—which led to three months of depression.

My mistake was in trying to validate my grief when all I had to do was say, "My dad died," and you'd already feel uncomfortable. I didn't need to invoke the feeling of grief or belabor the point. You already know. I also didn't want to imply that I'm "over the grief hump," because I'm not. I wanted to convey how my grief course-corrected a foundational part of me.

In this process, I've learned that a faith walk has similarities to the numbers "6" and "9." Both have the same shape, but what you see depends on your viewpoint. In the case of a faith walk, one path is fueled by fear of repercussions and condemnation, while the other is fueled by trust, joy, affirmation, peace and, most of all, love.

A Cup Left on a Table

By Lyda Michopoulou

IT TOOK ME 16 YEARS TO UNEARTH WHO I AM AND 20 DAYS TO lose myself.

———

I didn't know what was happening in the world, which was a first. Then, a friend messaged me asking if I knew what to do. As I plugged myself back in, I felt I was entering a nightmare. It was the week following October 7th, 2023, and I would come to learn that the state of Israel—in one evening—decided to annihilate all Palestinians living in the Gaza Strip. I remember feeling rage, anger, sadness, sorrow, immense guilt and shame. I saw people going about their typical day-to-day lives, and I wondered, "How on earth can you live your life when people are dying in Palestine?" Social media was worse. Most of my Instagram friends and followers cared more about the Israeli hostages and the fabricated stories about the many attacks attributed to Hamas but that had, in reality, been perpetrated by the state of *Israhell*.

As the days moved on, I found myself incessantly scrolling, sometimes for hours on end, trying to fathom the unfathomable. Having had enough Palestinian friends and discussions with them, I could empathize with their pain and sorrow. I decided to take a stand and speak up about Gaza.

I was called many names in private DMs such as "antisemitic," "Jew-hater," and others that I choose to forget. It hurts to know that people I met and connected with saw me this way simply because I spoke against the oppressor. What helped me to persevere and move forward was how emboldened I had become through PTSD therapy. The realization that *if I don't speak about injustice and genocide, no one will do it for me* rang truer than ever. The extreme emotions I experienced daily, though, whenever I was scrolling through my social media feed did take a toll on me.

———

Imagine you are able to connect with other people's emotions through any medium (screens, TVs, laptops, stories, discussions). Imagine seeing graphic images of bombarded hospitals, houses, refugee camps, dead children carried by their parents. Imagine knowing that in a not-that-distant corner of the world people die every hour. Imagine what that pain, sorrow, sadness, grief and guilt does to your soul.

And then, try to go back to your "regular" life. How?

———

In therapy, we say that a traumatic incident doesn't need to be ongoing and repetitive to traumatize (or re-traumatize) you. It simply needs just a moment where your body, soul, and existence is threatened.

It had been only four months since the end of my PTSD therapy, and it didn't take long for the vivid dreams and the restlessness to come back. Add to that feeling grogginess, sorrow and immense guilt and you have another traumatic experience waiting to happen.

To be clear, I didn't understand that I was being re-traumatized at the time. It was just another Tuesday with an ongoing genocide happening a few countries down and to the left. Apparently, my body understood that in order to avoid full-blown PTSD, something had to happen. And so it did.

Just like that, my body, soul and mind went numb.

———

For three weeks, life becomes a routine: waking up, checking my notifications and messages, spending time answering friends and followers who replied to my stories with two goals: 1. Trying to motivate them to post about the genocide happening in front of our eyes and 2. Supporting and holding each other while posting about Palestine.

I get dressed, drink some water, make my bed, put on

my shoes, take my laptop bag and off I go to my coworking space. Work, meetings, more work, some food in front of my laptop, more work. Around 8:30 p.m. I return home. At home, if I've finished my work for the day, I cook something easy and sit in front of my laptop to binge-watch one of the many series I have seen before.

This is the only way I know how to disconnect from this cruel, hateful world and enter a fantastic one. I am stuck there, usually until the early hours of the morning, until I have finished all seasons of the series I am currently (re)watching. When I feel brain-dead, I go to sleep.

This lasts for days on end.

In this state of numbness, I do things because they need to be done. Most of the things that are in my calendar are effortless; I don't need to come up with new ideas but follow a process I have followed before. These things will happen. I don't think about or do anything that needs soul, creativity, ideas. It's like those other things—writing a new chapter for my book, going to the theater, meeting friends, starting a new project—don't exist anymore.

Then, suddenly, I am pushed to re-enter the world of the living. My parents arrive unannounced in Athens, and I have to perform. I play the role of the put-together daughter, the one who has almost everything under control.

Being pushed into this fake role awakens me. I feel like I am emerging from a fog. It is a fog that has lasted 20 days where I truly and completely forgot myself.

———

Imagine you are drinking coffee at home. You love drinking coffee from your favorite cup and wherever you move within your house, you take that cup with you. Now, let's imagine something severe happens that shocks you to your core and you forget whatever else you were doing before. Your favorite cup is left on a table. Days pass and the cup is there, left on the table. You don't notice it. Your mind doesn't register it. It remains, without a thought. You keep drinking coffee from other cups without remembering you once even had a favorite cup.

Until the day, when somehow, brought back to reality, you realize the cup is still there. Left, forgotten. And you pick it up again, wondering how on earth could you ever forget it? It is your favorite cup after all!

———

I forgot my identity like a cup left on a table.

That's how it feels for me.

I forgot my nonbinary identity. I was emotionally and mentally exhausted until the moment I got out of the fog, and the realization hit me in the face.

How on earth did I forget?

Initially, this seems to be the big, scary truth for me: I forgot who I am. My mind cannot fathom the magnitude of not remembering who I am.

However, when I dig deeper, the biggest and scariest

truth is actually this: I got lost in my female-presenting persona and, if I am being brutally honest with myself, I got *comfortable* in that female-presenting persona.

The world was changing daily, and emotions were very heightened. But for those 20 days, I didn't need to speak up, fight for myself or fight for my right to exist.

When people saw me, they saw a female person. When they called me "Mrs., girl, lady, woman," I just let it pass. (Even with my own parents.) I didn't try to overthink or find a hidden meaning or something behind it. It felt slightly off and something inside me was pushing back, but I wasn't going to try to figure out what it was. After all, I was living in a placebo world. Similar to being placed inside the Matrix; I didn't know who I truly was deep down.

A few times, I was caught off guard when someone actually used my correct pronouns. I remember wondering, *to whom are they referring? Is there someone here who identifies as nonbinary?*

Oh, they mean me.

It's shocking, right? Or maybe not?

———

Generally, perhaps *not* shockingly, there are a few things I want to experience in this world:

- To walk down the street without looks from people trying to decipher what I am, asking, "Is it a man or a woman?"

- To be accepted by others without needing to prove that I have the right to exist.
- To not have to fight to be seen.
- To hear my correct pronouns, and to not have to fight for every little word.
- To be able to exist among others, just by being me.

But for 20 days, I left my nonbinary identity like a cup on a table and existed like most others do, no questions asked. I wasn't able to pick it up and wear it, so I used the costume society gave me when I was born. Within that costume, I felt a cringy freedom; I wasn't my truest self, but I didn't have to explain to anyone what my clothes imply or why my hair is cut this way or why I walk the way I walk.

I didn't have to decide if I should speak up every time someone misgendered me at the bakery or the supermarket. I didn't have to decide whether or not to correct a friend who hasn't yet "caught up" with who I am or a group of women-friends who make jokes and refer to all of us as "ladies" (ugh) or "guys" (even worse).

Because every single time I speak up and ask for what I need to exist in this world, the dignity and respect that is (or should be) a human right to call me with my name and correct pronouns/words I use, there comes a silence after.

A silence that feels inescapable, awkward, dense, heavy and suffocating. And after this silence comes the "I'm sorrys" and the distance; those people remember that I asked for something they don't know how to offer or don't want to offer. And they leave. And I am left alone, like a cup on a table.

What happens then? you might ask.

I pick up my pieces once again and figure out a way to make myself whole. And every time I pick up those pieces and try to stick them together, some might not fit anymore. Or something might be missing, lost forever.

But I persevere! What helps me move forward are elements such as going to therapy, talking to friends who see me, my full and truest self, venting on paper (a.k.a. writing), being immersed in nature, long walks by the beach, taking myself for coffee, and reading a book. In essence, doing activities that allow me to be myself and reconnect with the parts that have been broken. Healing the parts of me that were taken apart is painful. But I don't see any other way forward. If I decide to leave healing aside, I will become mean, vengeful, hateful, similar to the ones who took me apart so many times before. And that's not me!

And so, I pick up my pieces, heal myself and go on. Going back to wearing the cringy costume, my ex-female persona, full-time isn't an option. It's a prison, or rather a cage. A very tight cage where I feel myself slowly dying.

———

I recently found a page from my 2023 agenda where, amidst full-blown PTSD, I wrote the following:

Anger
      Rage
           Sadness
      Queer
White
      Non-binary
         PTSD
             Sadness
        Melancholy
     Who am I?

These words, written by my hand, feel both so familiar and so distant. Every time I speak up about my existence, a small voice creeps in asking, "Who are you, Lyda, really?" and the level of effort required to quiet that voice and keep on going varies greatly and depends on how any recent interaction went.

You see, when you question **my right to exist** as a nonbinary person either within the Greek or global society, I am placed in a position where I need to decide how to respond. Do I open a dialogue with you and try to educate you? To show you that, "Hey, I am a person too and I deserve to exist"? Do I dismiss you and your transphobic rhetoric? Do I find allies, others who support my right to exist and see me as an equal and are able to show you that what you are doing is harmful for all of us?

It depends on each situation, and it's not one-shoe-fits-all. But it's very exhausting.

I am called to make a split-second decision and respond (or not) to whatever transphobic slurs you decide to spew towards me. This constant alertness exhausts me, dims my radiance and darkens my soul. Negative thoughts swim in my mind and play on a continuous loop. I stand there unable to stop them, feeling incapable of getting back to where I used to be.

My invitation to you, dear reader, is to explore ways in which you can unlearn what society has taught you about nonbinary and trans people. Others continue to spew hateful rhetoric. Stop listening to them and see us for who we are: people!

Our differences don't divide us but make the world more colorful. It is a shame others diminish and try to erase us just because they think we are stealing their light. We aren't. There is space under the spotlight for all of us. (wink)

When others learn how to think, behave and speak towards us as human beings, as people who have the right to exist, then—and perhaps only then—will I be able to fully be **my truest self**; I wouldn't have to withdraw from my nonbinary self every time something truly destructive was happening in the world or hide parts or all of myself in hopes of waiting out the storm and once again unearthing myself. I deserve to be given the space where I am not forgotten, nor unknown to myself and others. But one where I'm able to bloom again and appear as **radiant** as ever.

Behind-the-Scenes

When I was first invited to participate in this project, I was overly enthusiastic. The first meeting with all the writers together, we were asked to think about what "success" looks like for us and the fears we have about publishing our piece.

It was far easier to list all my fears than to figure out what success would look like for me, but I managed. I think. Success for me is the moment I am holding this book in my hands and can share it with others. *See, my story matters. I matter.* Or, when I am able to add the author icon on my medium blog and Substack and celebrate all the steps that brought me to where I am today, among my fellow authors. Our words have finally been published to the world!

And now, the fears. First and foremost was my inability to sit down and write about anything in October 2023. Add to that my financial instability, my anxiety about money and not wanting to ask my parents to support me again, the sorrow and sadness I've been feeling for Palestine, and the depression I have been going through since March 2024 due to the hair loss I am trying to manage and accept. Mix in my fear of too much visibility and endangering my safety vs. my need and desire to share the essay I will write with others. Finally, pile on the uncertainty that has been looming around my life for close to a year now.

Besides, is there anything I'm even avoiding writing about? On the first few tries to put thoughts onto paper, I cannot think about anything that is holding me back or I am afraid of. I go through a list in my mind and scratch each thing off the list, saying, "Not this one, not this either, this seems small." I stare at a blank page, wondering what I should do to find what's holding me back. And then, it dawns on me: I am not going deep enough.

I start writing a few sentences explaining the background of my essay and after a lot of digging—and being very honest with myself—I arrive at the truly scariest truth. It's one of those moments that has happened to me only one other time, where I am writing and tears are suddenly running down my cheeks. It takes a lot of vulnerability to look yourself in the eyes, knowing deep down, *This is it, Lyda; you have found your truly scariest truth.*

As I embark on this writing journey, I feel anger, rage and frustration coming up. Anger because I am not able to just be me without being looked at like a freak by strangers on the streets. Rage because I live in a purely patriarchal society where the only two genders are male and female (which is bullshit). Frustration because there are people who say "you exist, you matter," and then take actions to show us that I don't.

Mixed among the rage, anger and frustration, there is guilt for not being strong enough to be out there and proud of being queer in all spaces. That brings me back to my fears. Fear of the unknown, fear of too much visibility, fear of being followed at night and attacked because I look "queer enough," fear of being attacked because I'm perceived as female, fear of just existing. And when I catch myself feeling afraid, the rage, anger and frustration return, and they are stronger. It's a mixture of emotions, all together, all circling around me.

And now, I have written my truth, gotten it down on paper. But there is my inability to end the essay. It's open-ended. And I wonder, do I *have* to close it? It just goes on. My life is ongoing, still happening. Why should I close the essay? I don't seem to like endings. I like situations that don't conclude. They simply exist and go on. And on.

Being Seen

By Asha Unni

"To be or not to be." In Shakespeare's *Hamlet*, the young prince of Denmark is deciding whether to live or die. For me, the question that has haunted me throughout my life is more complex: to hide or not to hide.

Existence can be undertaken in many ways. Does one remain in a quiet corner or dance into the limelight? Live out loud and take up space in a room, or become as invisible as possible? Mark a page or leave it in its pristine, white blankness—perfect, unsullied? While a mark may be ugly or laughable, making a mark means that you've taken a definite stance for the world to see.

In some ways, the question of hiding is a question of courage. Life is courage, every tiny bit of it. There is courage of the heroic kind that manifests in dire situations when one's survival is at stake. There is also the courage of everyday existence, of showing up despite the dark places in one's heart, despite the fear or sadness. Showing up even when you feel, or know, that you may be judged and found wanting.

However, the decision to hide or not to hide is not *just* about courage or lack of it. It is also about the peculiarities of one's personality. I, myself, have always been a person of contradictions, a person whose desires often pull in diametrically opposite directions, locking horns and paralyzing me into indecision. I have an innate inclination to hide and blend in that battles with an equally strong urge to show myself and be known. I want to express every bit of who I am. I want to quietly enjoy peace in my corner. I want to be like the cat, close to the hearth, sunning itself lazily. I want to be like the dog, bounding outside, greeting everyone with warmth and energy. I want to maintain an aloof distance yet be close to people. I want to sing and dance. I want the applause and attention. Yet the applause and attention are also torture, so I want to be left alone in peace.

I admire people who are free of such contradictions. They are quiet or shy and okay with being quiet or shy. They are loud and extroverted and perfectly content with that. Not so for me. If I am being quiet, I feel I should be outgoing, and if I am being gregarious, I feel I should be more reserved. When I was in college, I wanted to join in various sports matches yet hated being in front of people. I wanted to be in dance performances yet hated being seen. I wanted to write but could barely tolerate my words and thoughts out there for all to see.

I see them, the ones who dazzle easily. A smile here, a word there, a quiet, listening attitude. Something in them attracts others. In some, it is pure glamour. But in others, it is an intangible quality. What is it in a personality that makes for "popularity"? Some people make friends effortlessly, not necessarily due to any inherent goodness or accomplishment. People are simply drawn to them like bees to nectar.

Then there are others, like me, who struggle for connection. We are tolerated but not sought out. Observing others, watching how they behave, I have—chameleon-like—adopted their colors. I try on different shades, hoping one will do the trick, will fascinate or charm. Frustrated with my lack of success, I often decide to stop trying and just be me, to see if authenticity will change the dynamics. But which "me" shall I be? There are so many versions jostling to take center stage.

———

I have always been especially tuned in to other people's feelings, thoughts, and tone of voice. I grew up with an unconscious need to please people, to avoid offending at all costs. Yet, deep down, what I yearn for is to be freely myself without giving any thought as to how I appear to others.

From childhood, so much of what I felt inside was not reflected outside. I only revealed the bare minimum of who I was: the proverbial "tip of the iceberg." Over the years, I have slowly begun to let out hidden bits and pieces. I am learning to free myself of "oughts" and "shoulds," learning to accept myself and not feel so flawed, and learning to stop doubting my every action or inclination. No matter how great others think I am, I feel inadequate. I suppose there's a part of me that may always feel this way. As such, I cannot wait for these feelings to completely subside to do the things that I want to. I have to accept the contradictoriness of my nature. That's just who I am. If I have to go one way and then another, to constantly switch directions, then so be it.

So, I give up. Decide to just be. *Sink into awareness*, I tell myself. But the mind takes off on the wings of thought, carrying awareness with it. And I am lost. My consciousness is not grounded. It is too light, floating away with every changing direction of thought.

I post something in a WhatsApp group, and I am ignored. Being ignored hurts. Am I not sufficient enough for myself? Why the search for validation and acknowledgment? Yes, we are social creatures. But my yearning for connection goes deeper. Superficial positivity or social nicety does not satisfy me.

In *Lonely: A Memoir*, one of the people interviewed talks about how she will think about having people she can call and depend on and be around. "They can impose on me, I can impose on them, and we're just able to have a good time. But that's a daydream, that's the thing I make up in my head. In situations when I am with people, I find it…uncomfortable."* Another interviewee talks about the feeling of disconnection and asymmetry when it comes to fostering new relationships. This is similar to my experience. I keep wanting my gang, but I am unable to make

---

* White, Emily, *Lonely: A Memoir*. Harper & Collins, 2010.

that happen. All the people I know do not fit into this imagining or do not reciprocate to the same extent and depth that I seem to yearn for.

I want a group. *My* group. Is this a teenage fantasy?

———

Not being seen by others, I feel I don't exist. I don't matter. Is this what makes me dislike group chats or not getting a response? If everything exists only in relation to something else, this disappearing of me, this (non) act of not being seen, must mean I simply don't exist. Am I like a tree falling in a forest that nobody is around to hear? Who am I if my voice makes no sound? Even my writing is a way of escaping the feeling of being unseen, unknown, and unacknowledged.

Yet I often shy away from writing. Is it because I have nothing worthwhile to say, nothing of interest to others? I can feel a wellspring of thoughts and emotions bubbling inside, wanting to come out. Should I write only if I can get published or win accolades? Why not write just to write? To create and re-create sentences, carve a messy word path and keep fine-tuning it closer and closer to the place where my heart recognizes its aptness. Perfection is like infinity. You cannot reach it. Only directionalize yourself toward it and inch closer.

I started a blog once called "Innerspace" and posted one article. Almost immediately, I deleted the blog. Was it remnants of the painful shyness that paralyzed me as a teenager and young adult resurfacing? The fear of being judged and found wanting? I am no longer that person. Yet, I cannot say that person is no longer in me. We are, after all, made in the eyes of others. We are not separate, free-standing individuals but dyads, triads, tetrads, and so on. We are shape-shifters whose shape is dependent on the other.

———

Our earliest experiences seem to have the most profound and long-lasting impact on us. A blueprint from which we operate.

Little me hiding behind my grandmother's *mundu*, too scared to go to the two strangers who were my parents. They had come from England to claim me as their own and settle down as a family when I was three-years-old. But my family was my grandmother, and to have been torn away from her must have been sheer terror. The experience was akin to an earthquake shaking the core of my being. The next upheaval further damaged an already weakened foundation. I was five when I was sent to boarding school. When I think about it now, I cannot fathom why boarding schools exist for five-year-olds. At that tender age, your psyche is building your world for you. You need protection, security, indulgence, and to be the precious center of your family.

———

Is loneliness—and more specifically the desire to hide an inherited trait, a curse of a family lineage, or a coalescence of unfortunate circumstances—just the particulars of past Karma? Now, when I look back, I see that my father was lonely. He was a plastic surgeon who, after earning his degree in England, settled in a small town in Kerala, a place that had no use for his skills. In his heart, he was a philosopher whose inner leaning was toward teaching. Although circumstances had landed him with the prized status of a doctor, he did not find fulfillment in it. When I was young, I sometimes heard him pass a throwaway comment: "I have one foot in the grave. It doesn't matter." Or, "Sometimes I want to run away from everything." I never quite understood why he felt this way. It was probably just a venting of frustration, a temporary release that he didn't mean in the way it landed. But the words lodged somewhere in me, as did his pain. He was a volatile person—quick to anger and quick to recover after the storm cloud had passed.

My mother, on the other hand, is stoic, rarely expressing emotions, good or bad. She has no interest in my father's philosophical quest. I think of them as a volcano and an iceberg, an exaggeration that points to a truth. She stayed within the four walls of what was right, walking the straight path of duty. Her world was clear, obvious, and concrete. There was no room for magic or musings, for poetry or romance. For her, the numbers added up neatly and words were words; they meant what they were sup-posed to mean. I used to wonder whether under her prac-tical, efficient demeanor lurked some of the same turbulent emotions that coursed through me. Although we lived in the same house, we seemed to inhabit two separate worlds, tenuously connected by the thin thread of everyday real-ity. To her, I must have seemed alien. I am sure that she wished I were different, more "normal" and uncomplicat-ed. (Just as I wished she were different.)

I am certain I was a disappointment and probably caused her many sorrowful nights. I never seemed to feel the right emotions for the right people or at the right time. Outside events were a dim shadow compared to what was going on inside me. Marriages, births, graduations—events that meant so much to others did not hold my attention. They were the periphery of life. I lived inside with feel-ings, thoughts, fantasies, and imagination running wild, escaping the pain of the lonely misfit. What was inside struggled to come out. I wanted to be seen, really seen, for the person inside but was afraid of being judged and found wanting.

———

I project onto my son the feeling that he, too, is trapped in this endless cycle of loneliness and abandonment. I won-der if his fate is tied to this generational trauma. He is an introverted child whose father left when he was six. In the

United States, I am alone, away from my family of origin—a single parent, struggling to sustain a community of my own, yearning for closer friendships. I envy those large families who come to the park to play tennis, or a whole bunch of friends having lunch together, spread out across two or three tables. This is how a Saturday should be. Somehow, I could never make this happen. This family of belongingness and outings. I did not have the know-how or connections to make it work, and my desire to hide won out for so long. So my child grows up lonely without good family friends. This is what it feels like, never having "your people."

———

To hide or not to hide. Sometimes I'm not sure anymore where the siren's call is beckoning me. At both the beginning and the end of life, we seem to know and cleave to what matters most—the self in its purest form at the core, unconcerned with how it appears to others. We seek simple pleasures that nourish us, rather than flirt with grand ambitions or palatial desires stemming from vanity. We are content to live in the truth of what is rather than the incessant lure or the treacherous pull of what could be.

This is where I must find my home, in the grace of the present moment.

Behind-the-Scenes

I have scaled the walls of my discomfort all my life. Always pushing the edges a little further; in fact, to live meant pushing the edges, because everything was an edge for me. But if courage is not the absence of fear but the willingness to move forward despite it, then, in truth, I was—and am—brave, considering the number of worries I was assailed by, the fangs of which I had to face and overcome. I traversed the razor-sharp edge of my discomfort so many times, it felt like I was living on a precipice.

I assumed I was a coward because every little thing frightened me. While people often talk about trying something new and daring to expand their comfort zone—as an occasional adventure—my life was a constant challenge. My comfort zone was so narrow that practically everything felt outside of it. Every day was about stretching and pushing my limits.

I have survived so much, endured so much. Anxiety is the twin of my every desire, creating a tug-of-war in my psyche. Thus, pulled taut by equal and opposing forces, I am often unable to decide whether to move toward my desire, despite my fear, or heed its warning and stay away.

But here we are. I have presently arrived at a stage in my life when showing myself seems more urgent than staying hidden to avoid being judged. I want the world to know who I am, not what they think they see, but deeper, before it's too late. It seems that if I can be fully myself without fear or shame, then life has some meaning. So I strive to be brave and lay it out there.

It's still scary! One must plunge in without too much debilitating thought. Somewhere deep inside of me, there's a little girl who hid herself in order to survive. She's been there all along and she's still hiding. In every environment, she donned different roles, scanning those around for clues so she could fit in and act just right so that she would not be found out. She became a master of disguise, a chameleon, a finely tuned antennae of other people's tones, emotions, and judgments. Always feeling like a fraud, one who no longer knows her own voice or being. A road laid waste with potential never realized. Now, that little girl is trying to show herself, to make up for a lifetime of invisibility before it is too late.

Acknowledgements

First and foremost, thank you to the 13 contributors of this collection. Your willingness to jump into this project, your patience with the process, and your trust in allowing me to hold your stories has been received with so much gratitude.

Thank you as well to the entire Open Book Community, past and present. Our little Zoom writing group has become a liferaft for me over the past four years. You all motivate me, inspire me, and keep me going.

This book was a labor of love by my entire team. Thank you to our interior designer, Nicki Pappas, for bringing your patience (with me) and commitment (to this project). Your attention to detail has greatly enriched the final stage of this book's creation, my friend. Thank you to *my* copyeditor—yes, editors need editors—Pamela Toussaint, for your collaboration and cheerleading, and to our cover designer, Deja Brown, for your creative vision and supportive energy.

A special thank you to Maria Wade for (sneakily, gently and lovingly) nudging me until I remembered what types of leaps I am capable of making. With immense gratitude, also, to those who see me, are always honest, and listen to my lengthy voice memos.

Finally, thank you to my family for your unwavering support (and songs and laughs).

About the Authors

Katie Boateng (she/her)

Katie is from Cypress, Texas and helps run the Smell and Taste Association of North America, a national nonprofit focused on smell and taste dysfunction. She loves yoga, reading, and hanging out with her family. Katie haphazardly writes in snippets during her children's naps and after bedtime. She dreams of sleeping the entire night without waking up and traveling the world with her family.

Federica Bruniera (she/her)

Federica is a messy, disorganized, socially anxious, and permanently uncombed human.

She's addicted to travel and, after living in Italy, France, Japan, Canada, and Colombia, she gave up any desire to settle down. She lives with a backpack on her shoulders, never taking up more than two drawers' worth of space anywhere. Black belt in tripping over nothing and stubbing her little toes, when she pretends to be a functional adult, she is a translator from English, French, Spanish and Japanese into Italian. Writing is her way to make sense of the world, so she keeps starting new projects: a travel blog—*The Globetrottoise*—with a newsletter attached, an epistolary Substack called *Letters from the Road*, an upcoming travel memoir about her Panamerican journey in her minivan, and a bunch of social media accounts.

She's an advocate for sustainability and environmental justice, and in her free time she volunteers as a facilitator for a variety of educational workshops on climate change, biodiversity, the circular economy, and sustainability. She dreams of traveling the whole world and writing about it. She loves the ocean and has a hyper-fixation with turtles— so much so that her crocheted turtle, Matilda, never leaves her side. She doesn't like chocolate, so she can't be taken too seriously.

Connect with Federica: @federica.globetrotthuman and @globetrottoise.

Becka Eppley (she/her)

Becka is a writer and speaker specializing in authentic storytelling and connection, based in Charlotte, North Carolina. A lifelong storyteller, she helps individuals, nonprofits, and communities express their voices with clarity, creativity, and heart. She currently serves as Communications Director for a local nonprofit and is the founder of Becka Eppley Media, where she supports authors, coaches, and community builders in sharing their truth.

Her personal writing lives at *A Mile Deep*— beckaeppley.substack.com—where she explores identity, spirituality, love, and resilience in times of upheaval. Becka also co-facilitates work with The Allgood Collective, a community of practice, helping people and organizations navigate change, repair harm, and grow through curiosity, embodiment, and care.

Coming out later in life as a lesbian transformed Becka's understanding of truth and belonging. Raised in an ultra-conservative Southern Baptist and Christian nationalist home, she spent decades untangling religious conditioning and reclaiming her authentic self. Writing became her way through—naming what was once silenced and finding freedom in her own voice.

A mom of two growing humans and a lover of spoken word, embodiment practices, and deep community conversations, Becka believes storytelling—raw and honest—is a practice of becoming; a way we learn to give permission to ourselves and to one another.

You can connect with Becka on most social platforms @BeckaEppley.

Serine Goodmond (she/her)

Serine is a facilitator and strategist who designs transformative experiences and builds systems that help people thrive. With over seventeen years in business operations, she has guided entrepreneurs, small businesses, and early-stage companies in creating clarity, structure, and strategies that stick.

Beyond operations, Serine has spent nearly a decade facilitating programs across diverse settings—from men's maximum-security prisons to creative studios and leadership teams. Trained through the Alternatives to Violence Project, she founded *Shift from Shame*, a platform dedicated to disrupting the ways shame constrains our choices and connections.

Her work is rooted in the belief that authentic connection fuels transformation. Whether streamlining operations or leading vulnerable dialogue, Serine creates spaces where people can relate more deeply, grow more freely, and lead with greater self-awareness.

Connect with Serine on LinkedIn @serinegoodmond or Instagram @shiftfromshame.

Amanda Conley Hines (she/her)

Amanda is based in Michigan. In addition to being a fiction writer, Amanda is a wife, mother and Navy Veteran who loves to read, camp, travel, diamond dot and crochet. Amanda currently shares her love of writing through episodic fiction. Connect with her on Substack @storiesofamosaicmind.

Kim Marsh (she/her)

Kim is the curator, editor and publisher of this anthology. A writer, editor and writing coach, she founded The Open Book Company with the deeply held belief that you don't need a major book deal, a spot on a global stage or a PhD in English Lit to have a story worth telling. She recently launched Plymouth James Press, an independent imprint, to further support authors on their publishing journeys.

You can connect with Kim on Substack @openbookco, via The Open Book Company website, or on LinkedIn.

Jinx Malcolm (they/them)

Jinx spends a lot of time lately working with mutual aid groups. They love nature and hiking! Jinx feels their soul is the most at peace with their feet on a trail, especially with their dog, Flo. They love to *actually* hug trees, imagining what it might feel like to reach towards the sun with an outstretched hand of leaves. It is calming and allows them to feel the flow of connection between loved ones and the connection between everything from the earth to the universe. They highly recommend hugging a tree.

Jinx's writing comes from the inspiration of dozens of authors, including the people involved in making this book! When they read or hear an author create a piece that generates an electrifying experience, or a mind movie, they try to imitate that. Jinx is especially inspired to write horror, as they feel it is a genre that allows deep reflection of what holds us back the most. Naming our curses gives us a bit more power over them.

Jinx can be found on Substack @jinxmalcolm, Instagram @craftyhijinxm and @sudbudsco and on Tik-Tok @sudbudsco.

Lyda Michopoulou (they/them)

Lyda is a queer, nonbinary writer, speaker and professional life coach. Called by life itself, their curiosity into the creative world has been inspired by the innate beauty within it; they have been on a journey of exploring what it means to shape the world, personally and collectively. This journey has taken them from Canada to Chile and from Portugal to Turkey, each location an opportunity to hear their heart calling in the power of stories, both spoken and written, and to find collective liberation through coaching and writing.

Lyda is a trauma-informed professional who works with folks who feel anxious and uncertain about transitions in gender identity, relationships, and lifestyle. They are neuroqueer (ADHD and cPTSD) and understand that everyone's processes and understanding are different. Lyda fiercely believes in inclusion and through their work as a coach, Lyda strives to create a brave space, so their clients feel safe to show up as their truest self—no limits. When they aren't writing, Lyda likes to go on long walks by the beach, loves the smell of damp soil after the rain and gets excited looking from their window at the shapes lightning makes during a storm.

Connect with Lyda on Instagram and Substack @unwrappedevolutions.

Nicki Pappas (she/her)

Nicki is an author, podcaster, and actor. More than all of this, she is a human being learning to "relax toward the things that feel possible" (according to the Co-Star astrology app). Her books include the memoirs *As Familiar as Family*, *Becoming Egalitarian*, and *Coming of Age and Coming Out* and the poetry collections *Reflections from a Former Evangelical*, *More Reflections from a Former Evangelical*, and *Fi-*

nal Reflections from a Former Evangelical. Nicki was the host of the *Broadening the Narrative* podcast, where she connected with people who are broadening the narratives she was taught within white evangelicalism; she started the *So You Think You Can Date* podcast to share her adventures in dating as a queer, poly, millennial mom who started dating again for the first time in fifteen years.

Her newest endeavor involves reconnecting with her first love: the theater. As part of a local company, she regularly acts and has written, directed and produced numerous plays. She is also the Director of Self-Publishing at The Open Book Company. Through all of her work, she desires to spark hope, healing, and whole human flourishing in the world around her.

Connect with Nicki on Instagram and TikTok @broadeningthenarrative and on the *Coming Alive* Substack @nickipappas.

Tina Strawn (she/they)

Tina is a writer, retreat curator, joy and liberation activist, racial and social justice advocate, and author of *Are We Free Yet? The Black, Queer Guide to Divorcing America.* She has a TedX Talk entitled, " Blaxit: The New Underground Railroad."

The heart of Tina's work is founding, hosting and leading Legacy Trips, immersive and all-inclusive experiences that center embodied practices and collective liberation work such as grief and healing, peace and pleasure, joy and celebration, and activism and liberation, in places like Alabama, Jamaica, Ecuador, and Costa Rica. Tina has three adult children, an ex-husband, an ex-wife, and an ex-country. She has been a full-time minimalist nomad since February 2020 and currently lives and loves in Costa Rica with her three jungle cats.

Connect with her and view *The Are We Free Yet? Files* on Substack @tinastrawn.

Therese Temitayo (she/her)

Therese is a part-time worker from New York, NY. When she's not working, she spends her time writing, baking, and being silly. She currently lives in Belgium, exploring (read: eating) to her heart's content.

You can follow her on X(Twitter) at @ss__map or Instagram at @ss.map.

Asha Unni (she/her)

Asha, originally from Kerala, India, is a Library Services Manager in New York with a background in Indian classical music and dance. She enjoys group singing, theater, and writing, and is particularly interested in family dynamics, relationships, and the psychology of loneliness and connection. Through her short stories, poems, and personal essays, Asha explores societal expectations and the hidden motivations of people.

You can read more of her work on her Substack, *Ripples in Silence*.

Laura Vegh (she/her)

Laura is a writer and content strategist with a background in academia and cybersecurity research. After earning her Ph.D., she shifted paths to pursue writing full-time, first in the world of B2B content and eventually through personal essays that explore vulnerability, resilience, and the quiet strength it takes to start over.

She's passionate about telling stories that live in the in-between spaces: between certainty and doubt, fear and courage, silence and expression. When she's not writing, you'll usually find her walking without a destination, playing chess, rereading old favorites, or trying to convince herself to finally take a real vacation.

You can read more of Laura's stories on Substack @lauravegh or on LinkedIn.

Maria Wade (she/her)

Maria is a leadership coach, speaker, and author of *Leadership Integrity Framework: How to Stay Grounded, Build Trust, and Lead with Wholeness in Uncertain Times*. She works with senior executives navigating complexity, helping them lead with more clarity, courage, and compassion.

Maria's journey across borders, languages, and cultures informs both her coaching and her writing. English is not her native language, but it is the one she writes in now, one word and one act of bravery at a time. Each sentence represents not just communication but a deliberate choice to be understood across the spaces between worlds. She doesn't believe in writing to impress; she writes to connect. Her words explore resilience, identity, and the uncomfortable—but liberating—process of being seen. She believes that writing isn't about being a "real writer," it's about telling the truth you're finally ready to live.

As a mom of twins who recently left for college, Maria is discovering that empty nest syndrome comes with unexpected gifts—more time to write and deeper wells of emotion to draw from. Her essays emerge from the intersection of professional expertise and personal evolution, where technical skill meets the courage to reveal what matters most. She writes because not writing is no longer an option.

Connect with her (mariawade-coach) on LinkedIn.

The Open Book Company

Connect with The Open Book Company
(& our writing community)

www.openbookco.com

PLYMOUTH JAMES
PRESS

Plymouth James Press is an independent imprint
of The Open Book Company.

With an "author first, book second" path to
publishing, we emphasize the power of human-to-
human, personalized connection in the storytelling
process and pride ourselves on transparency and ethics.
We are a values-driven house, publishing books with
meaning and a message.